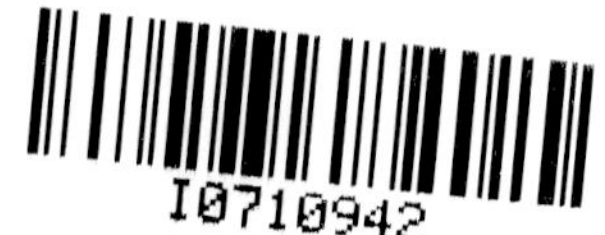
I0710942

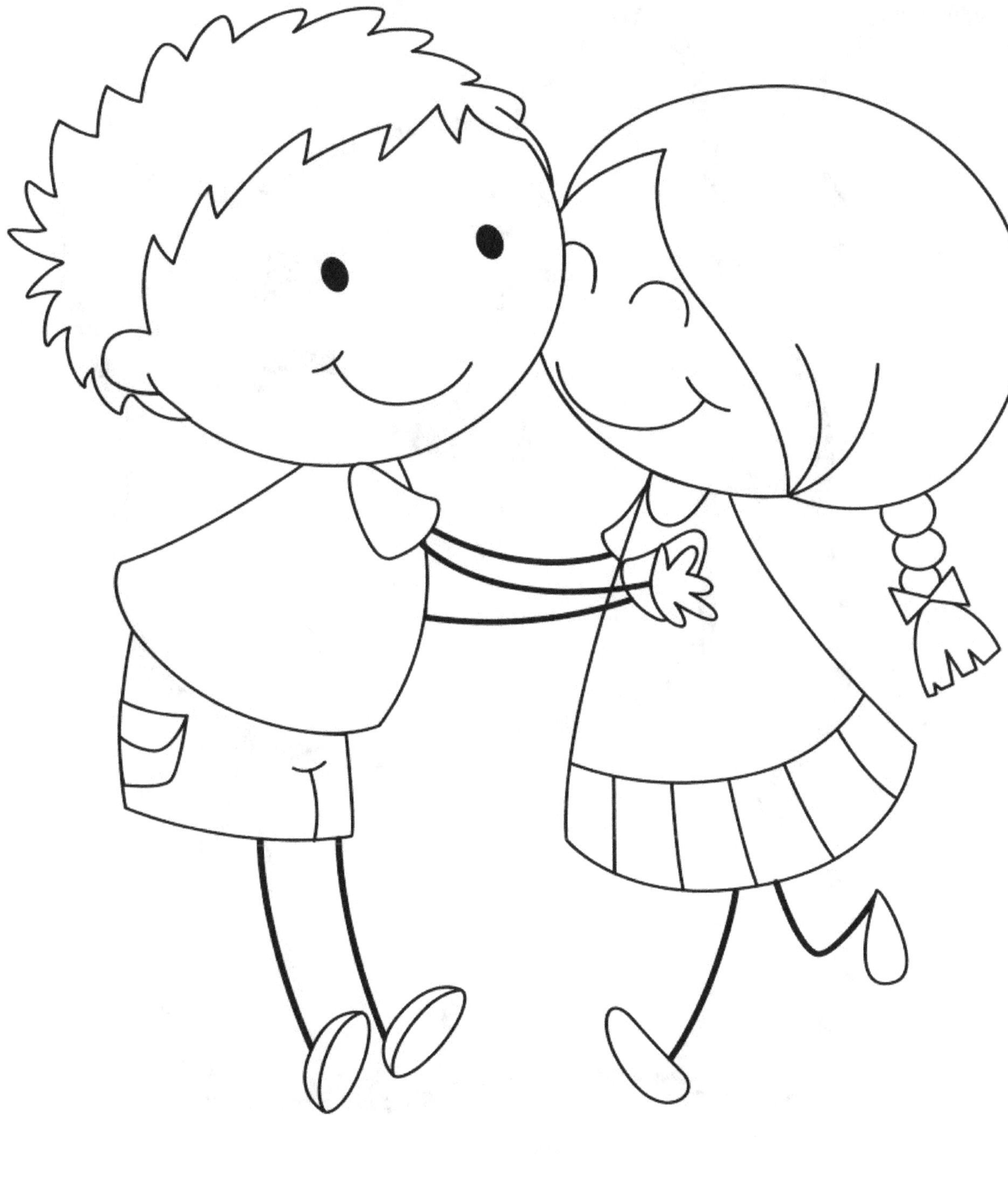

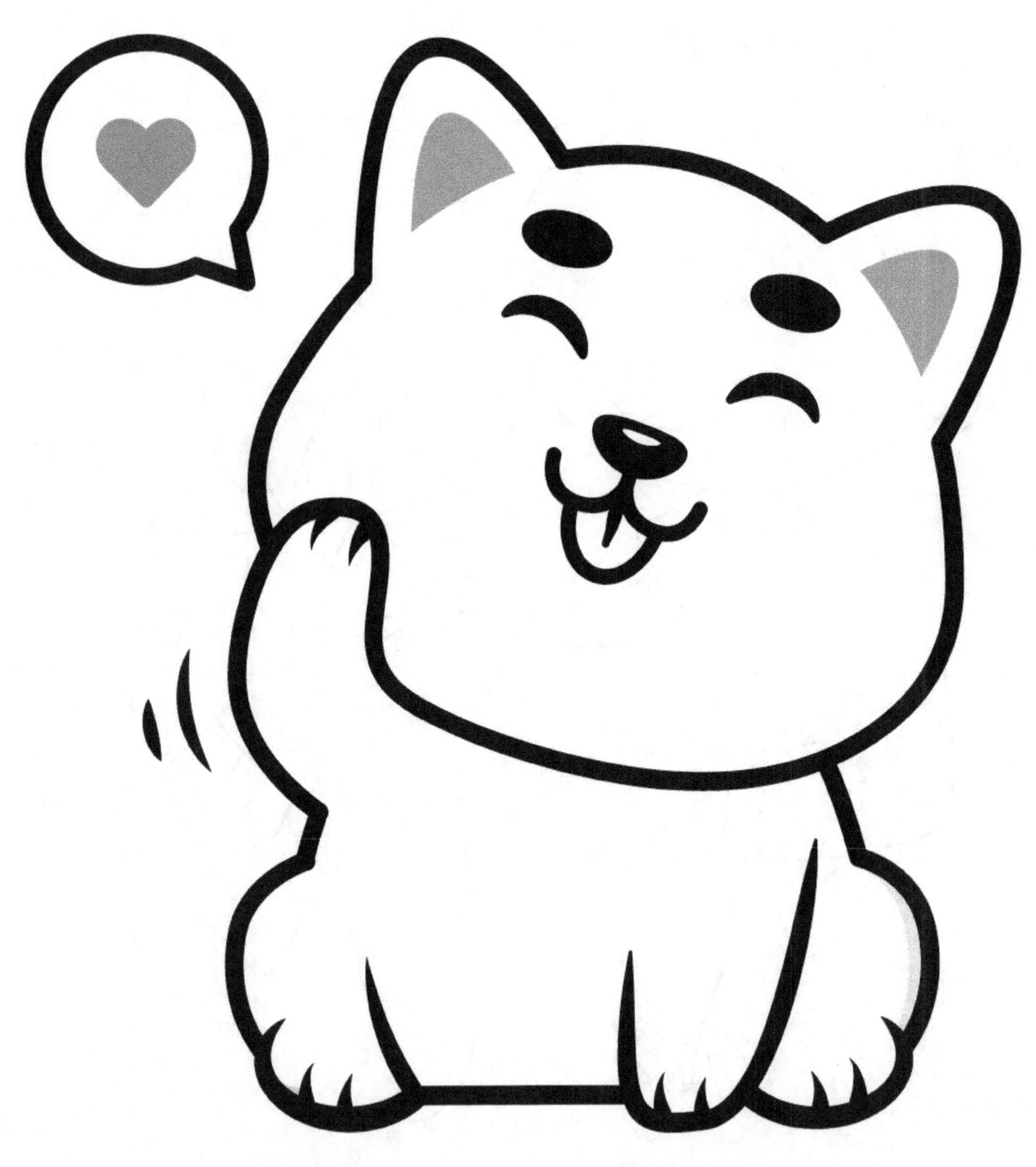

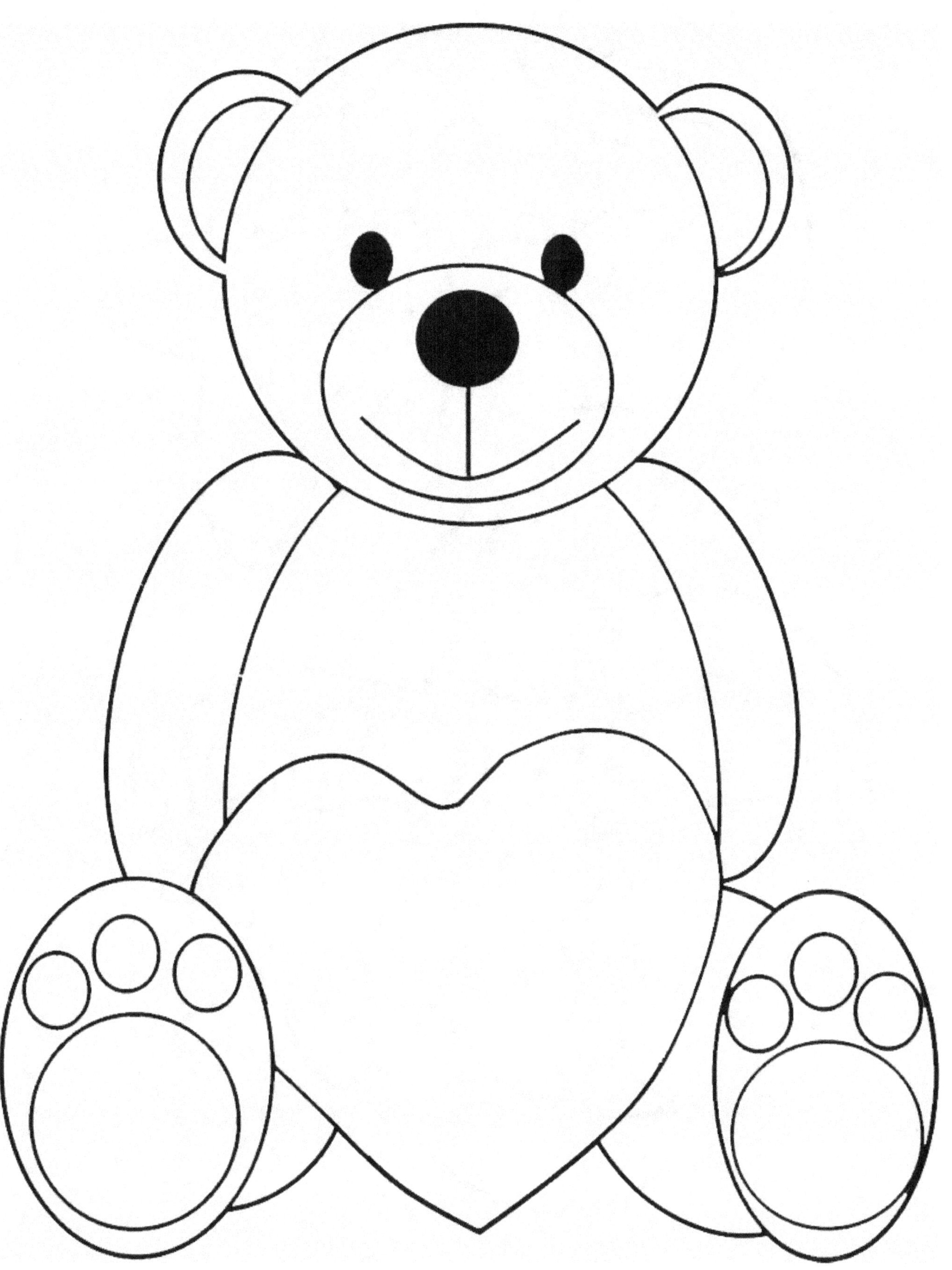

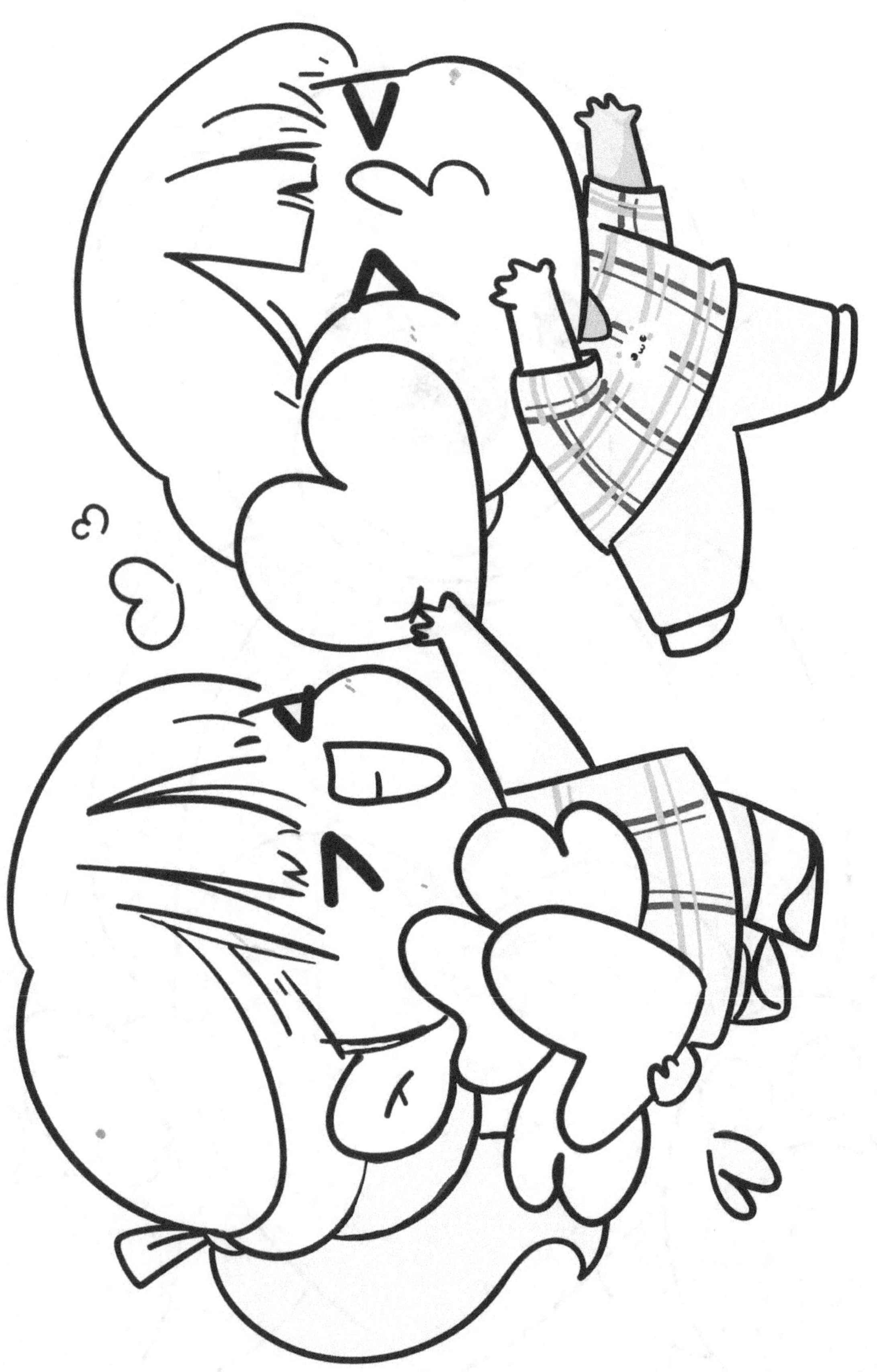

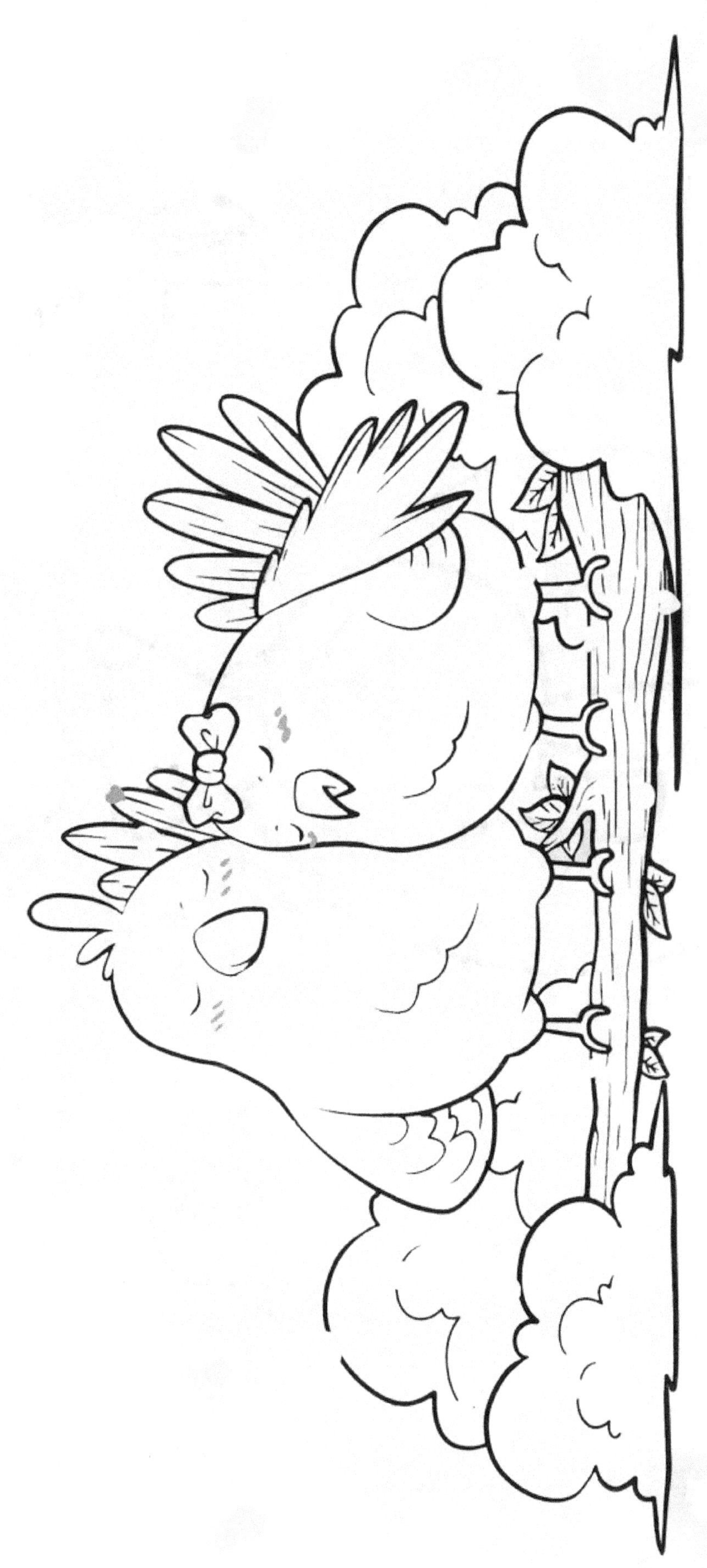

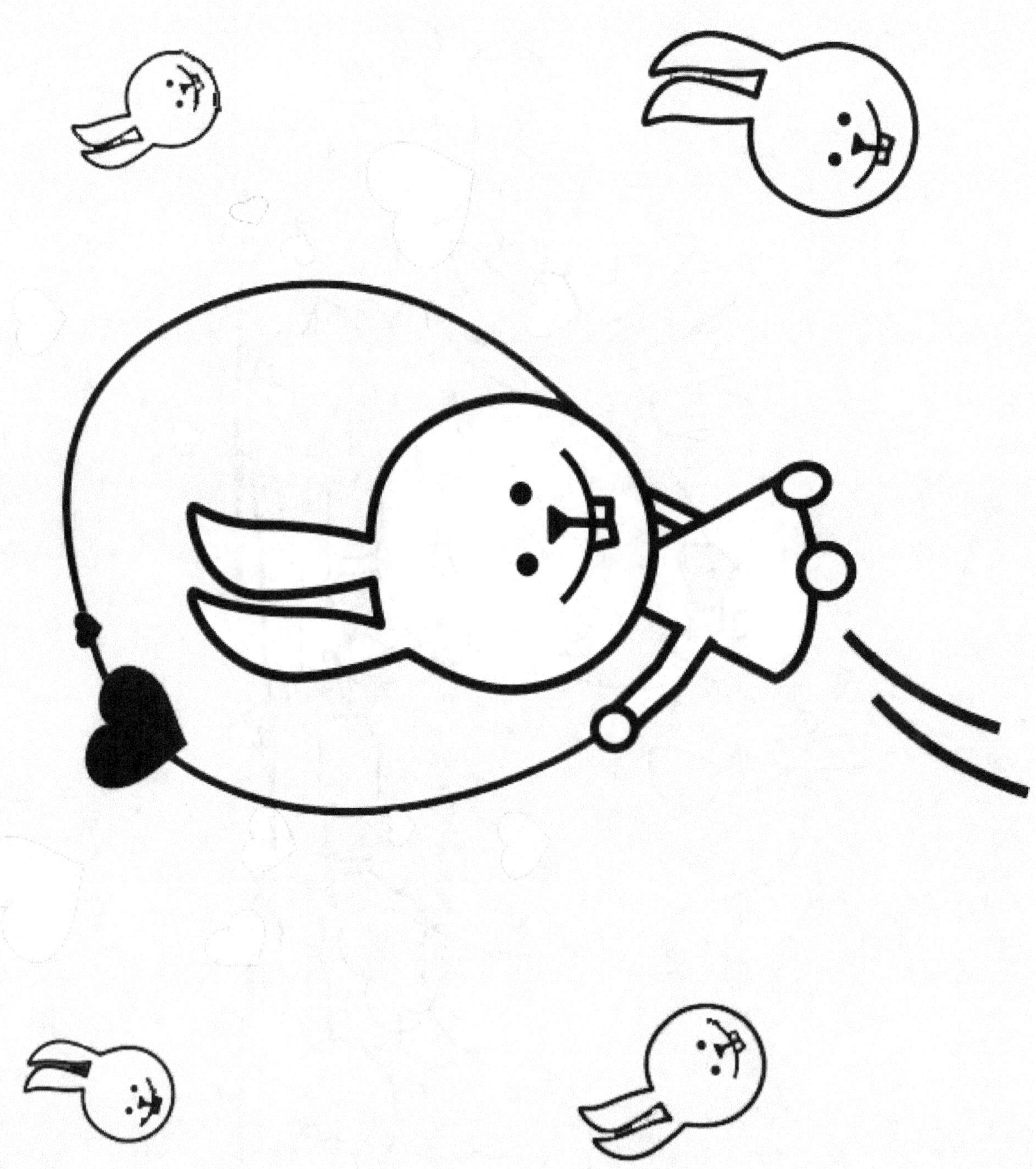

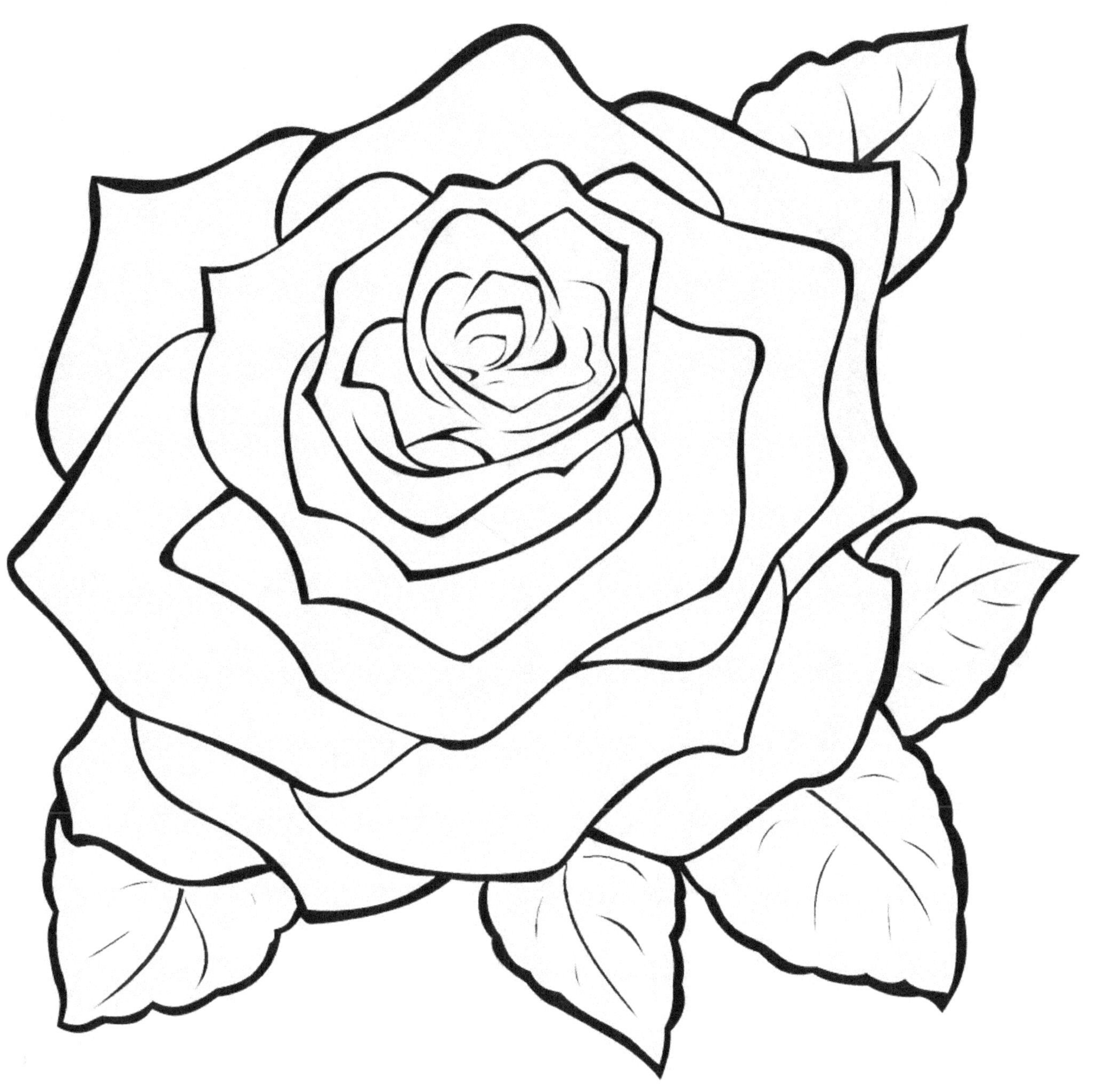

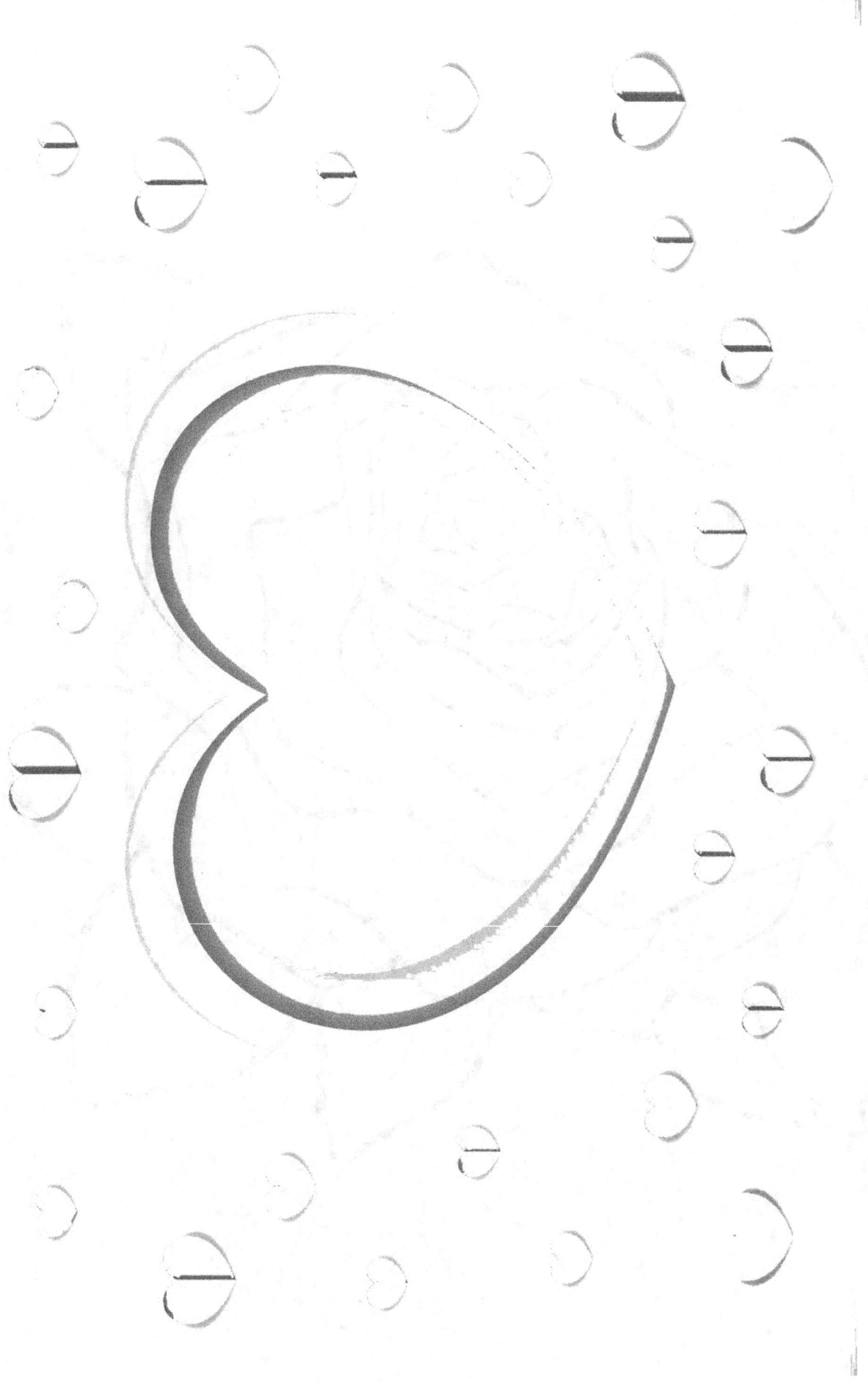

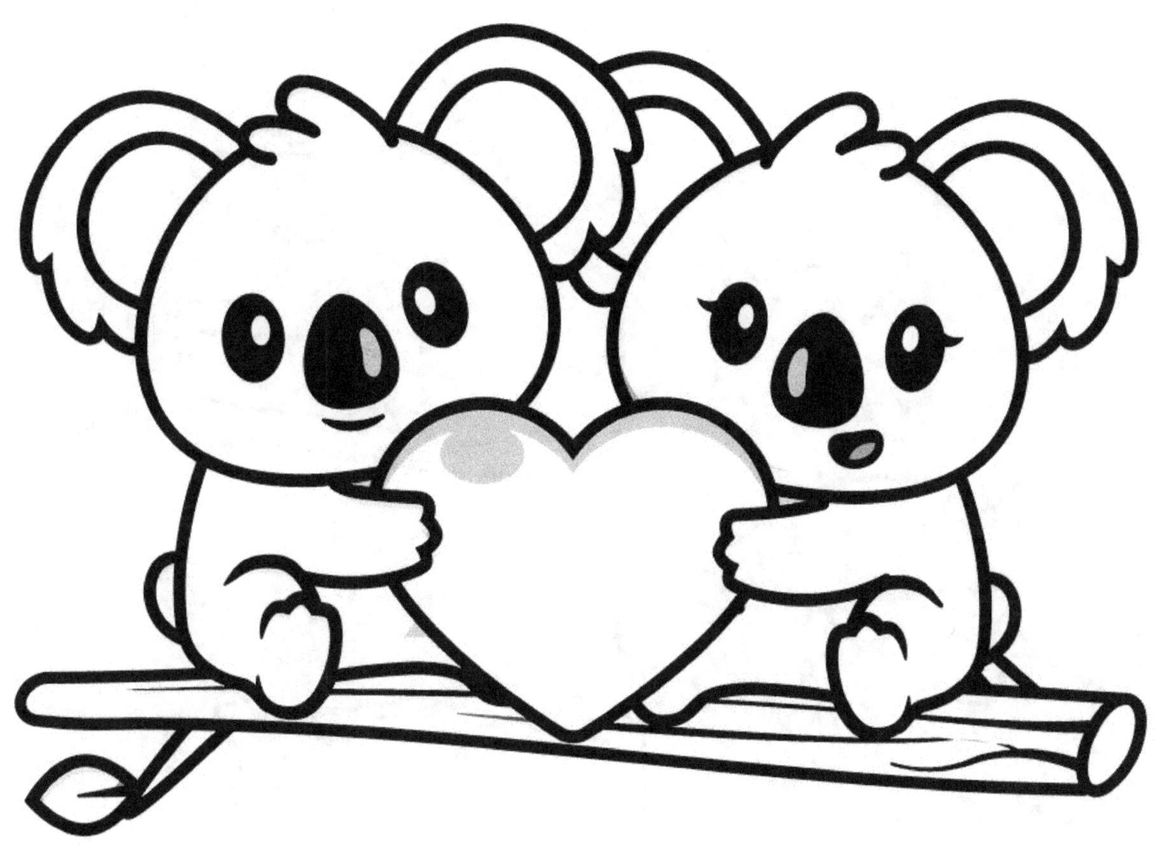

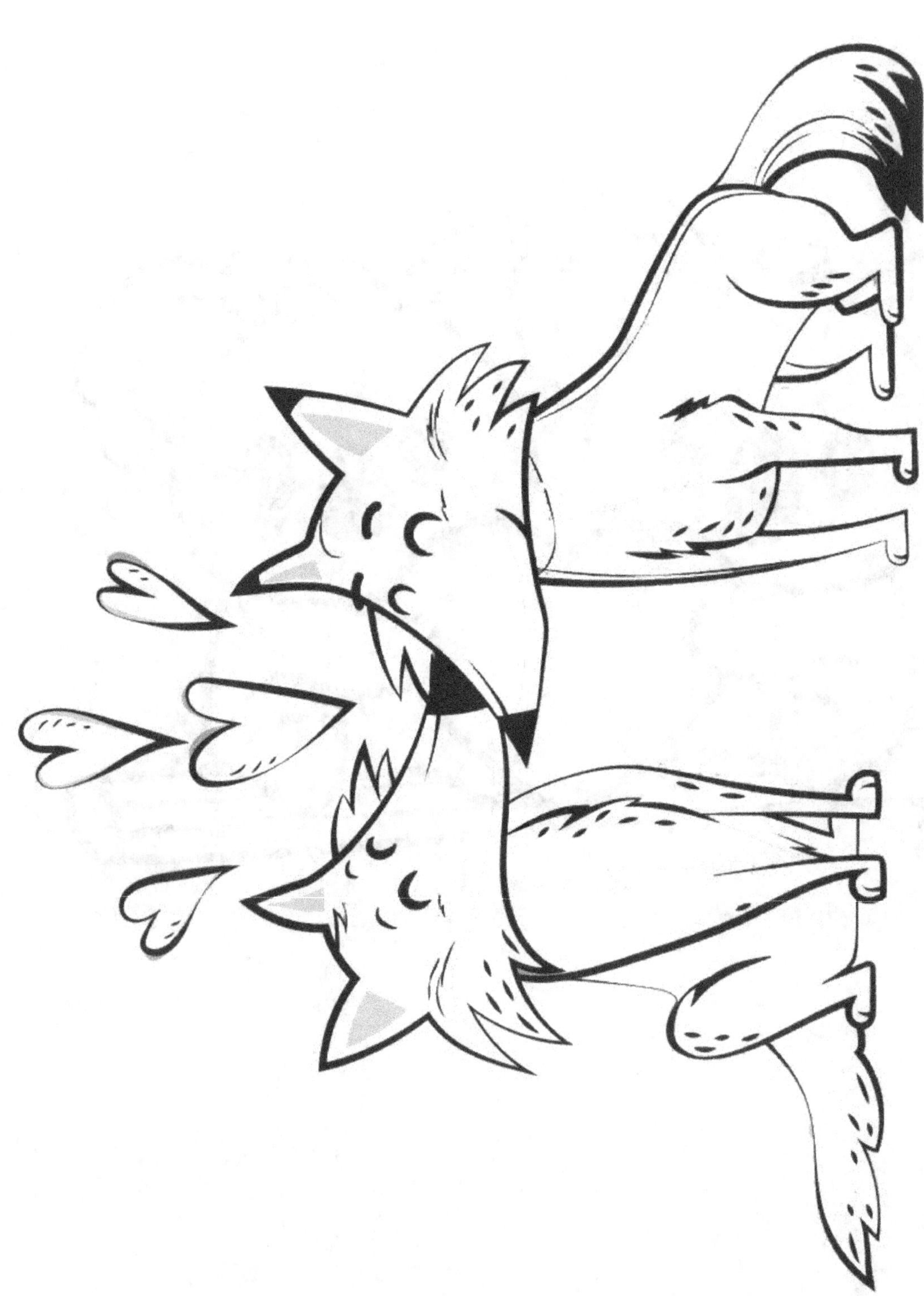

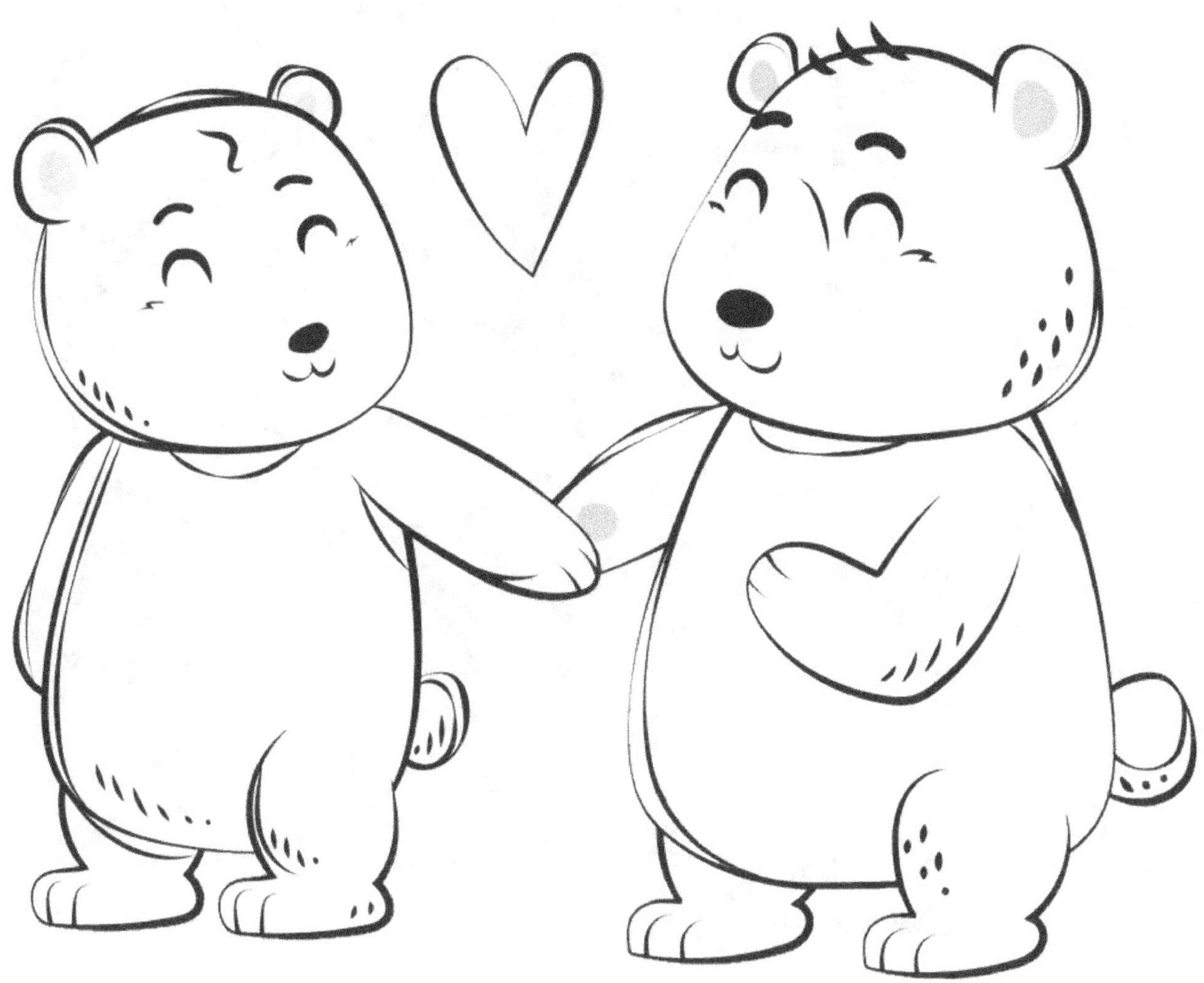

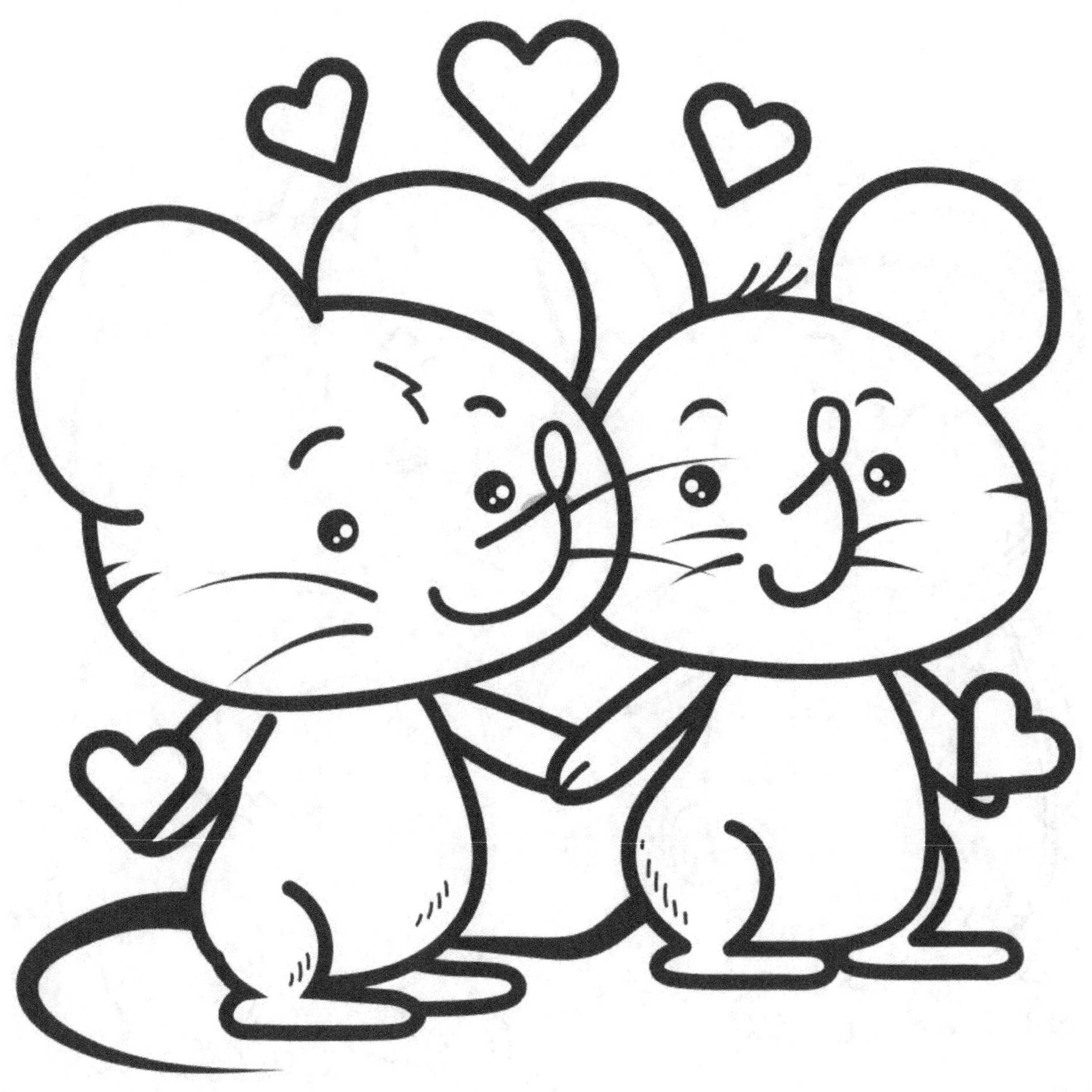

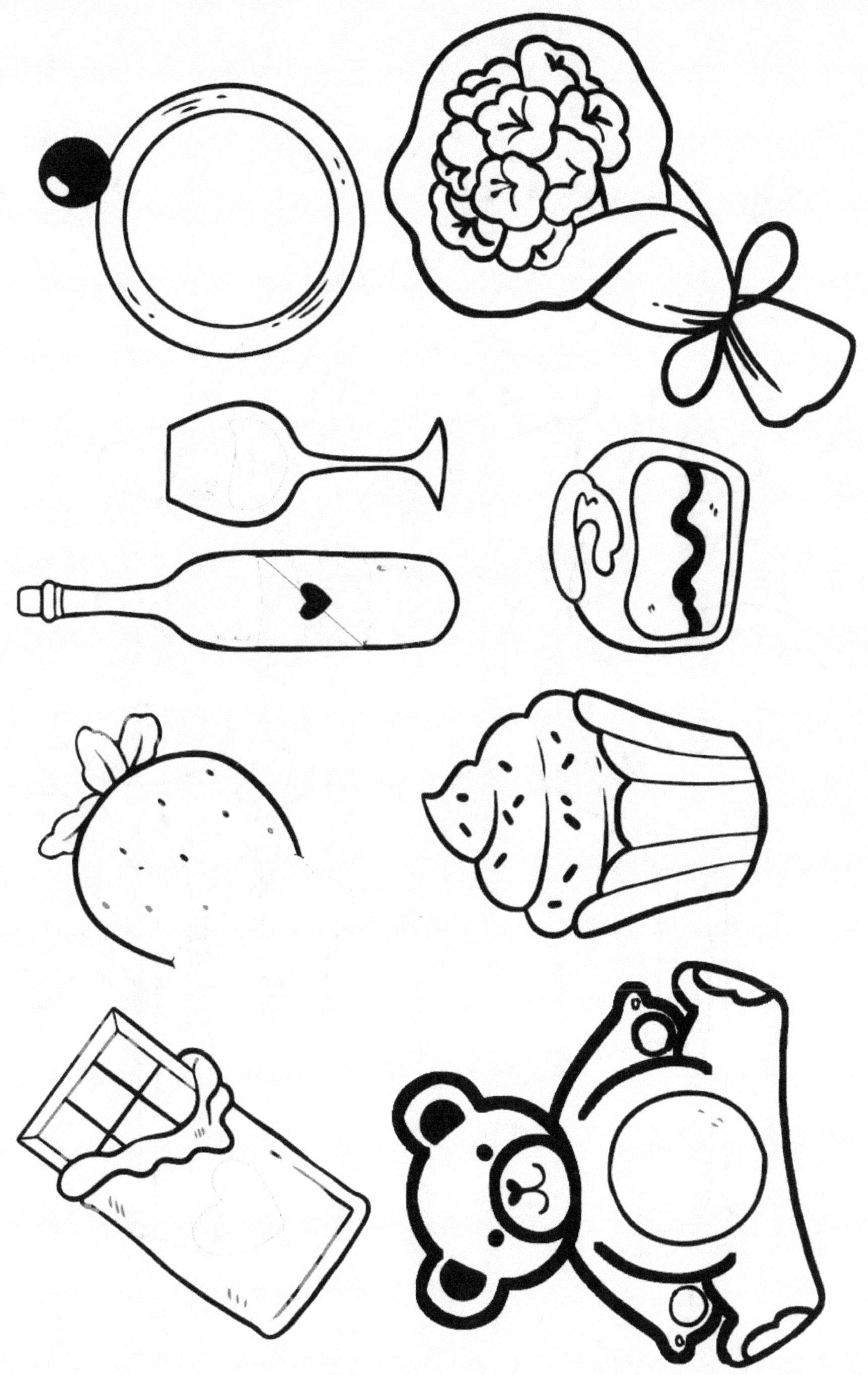

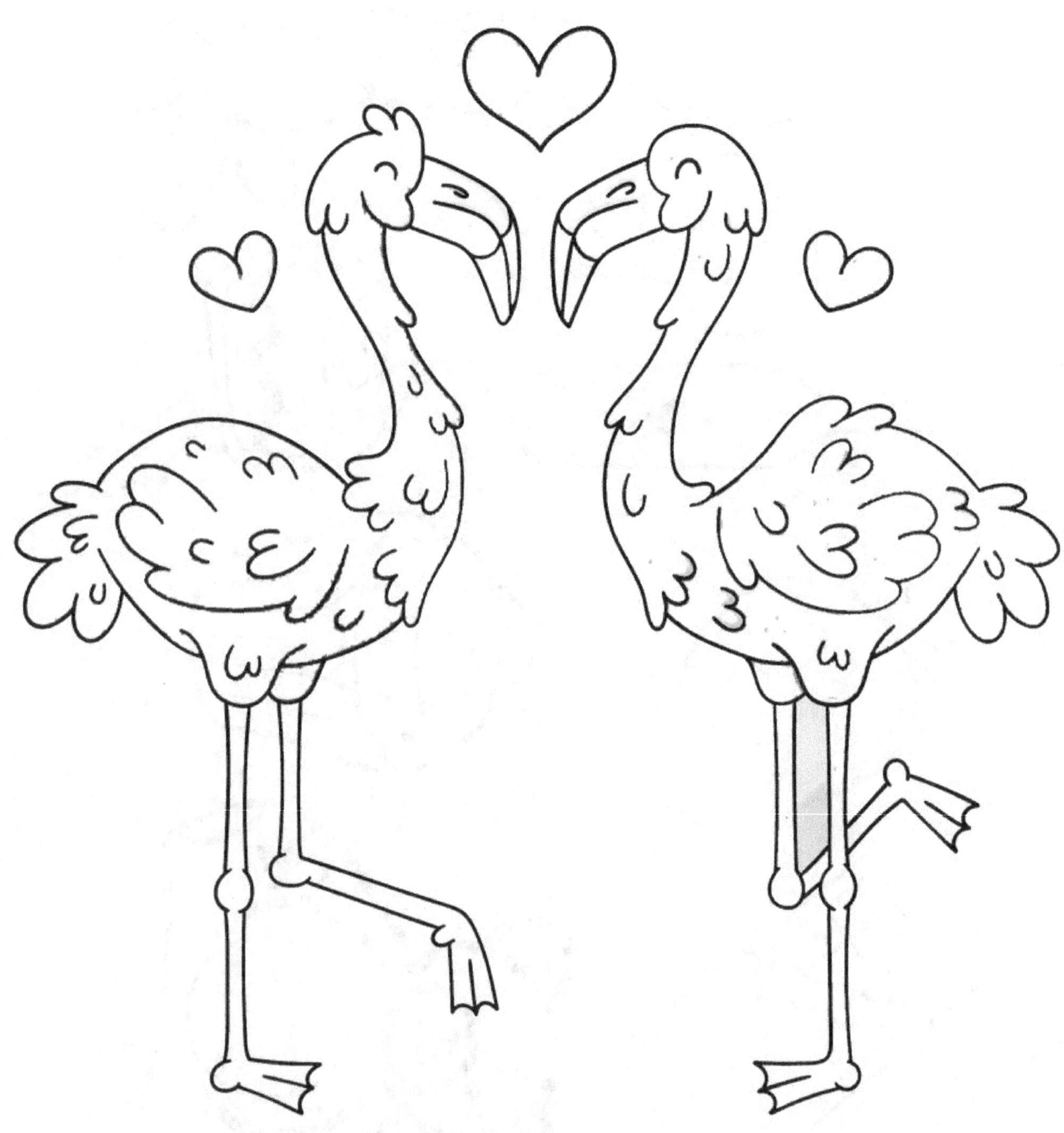

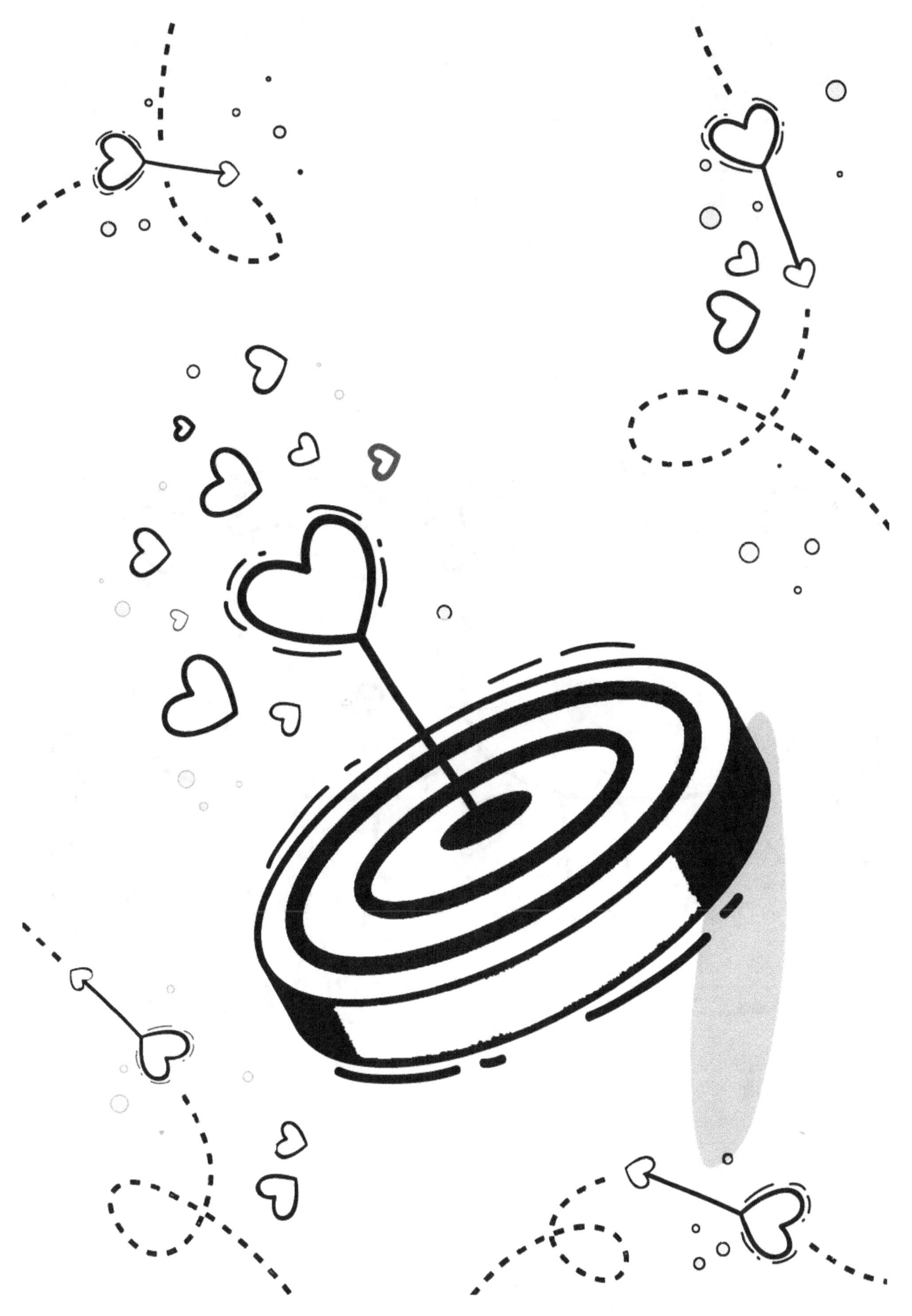

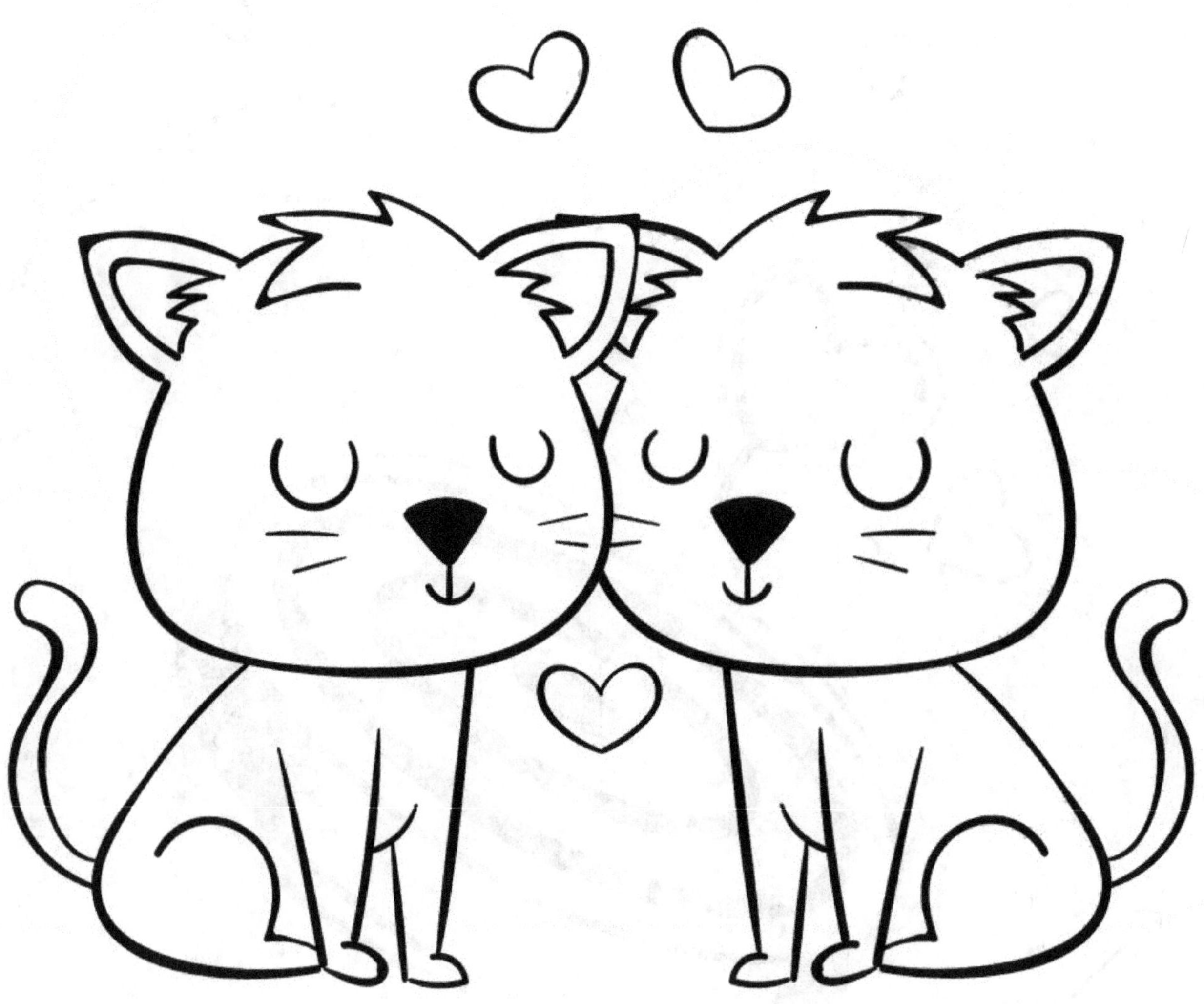

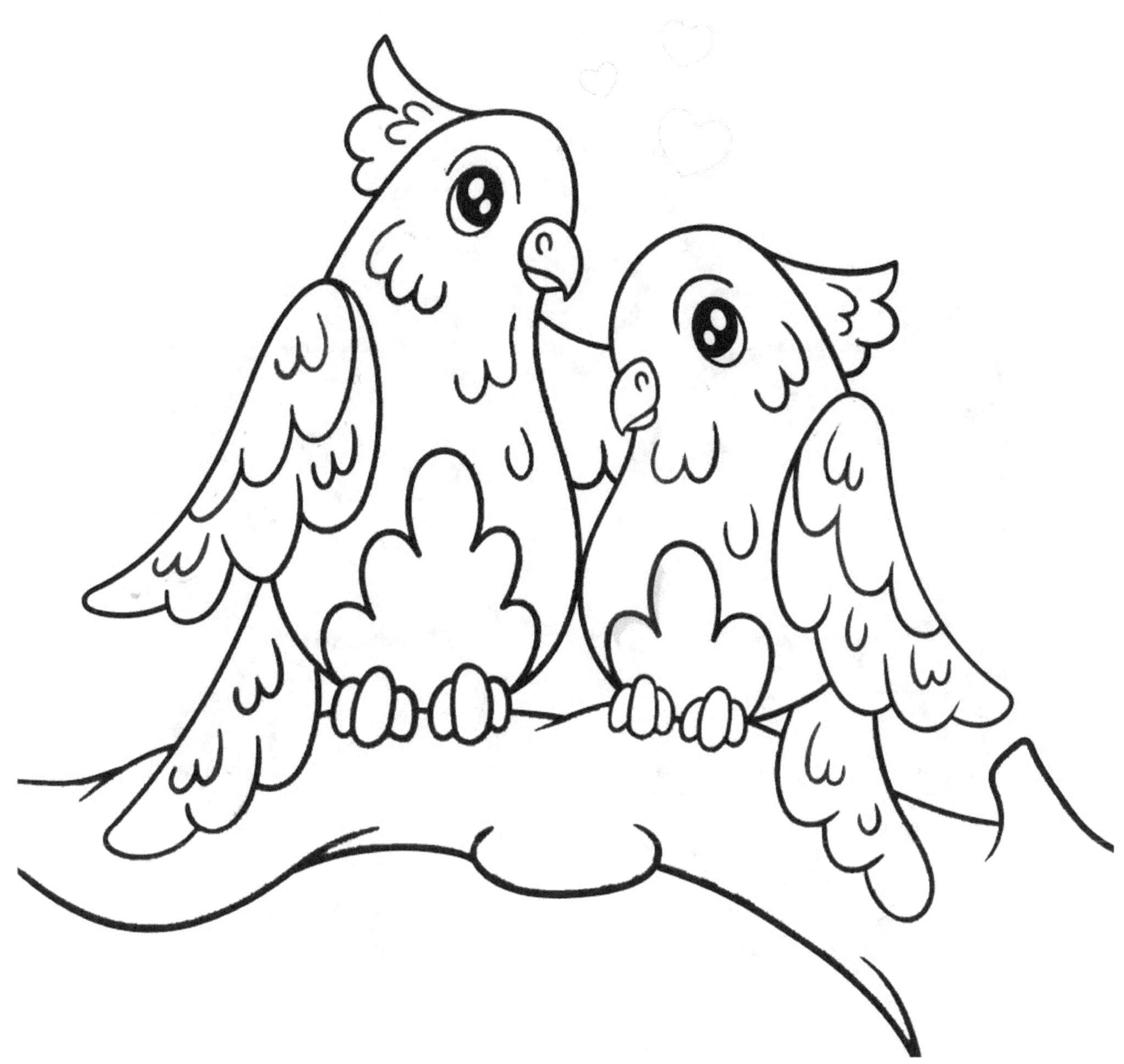

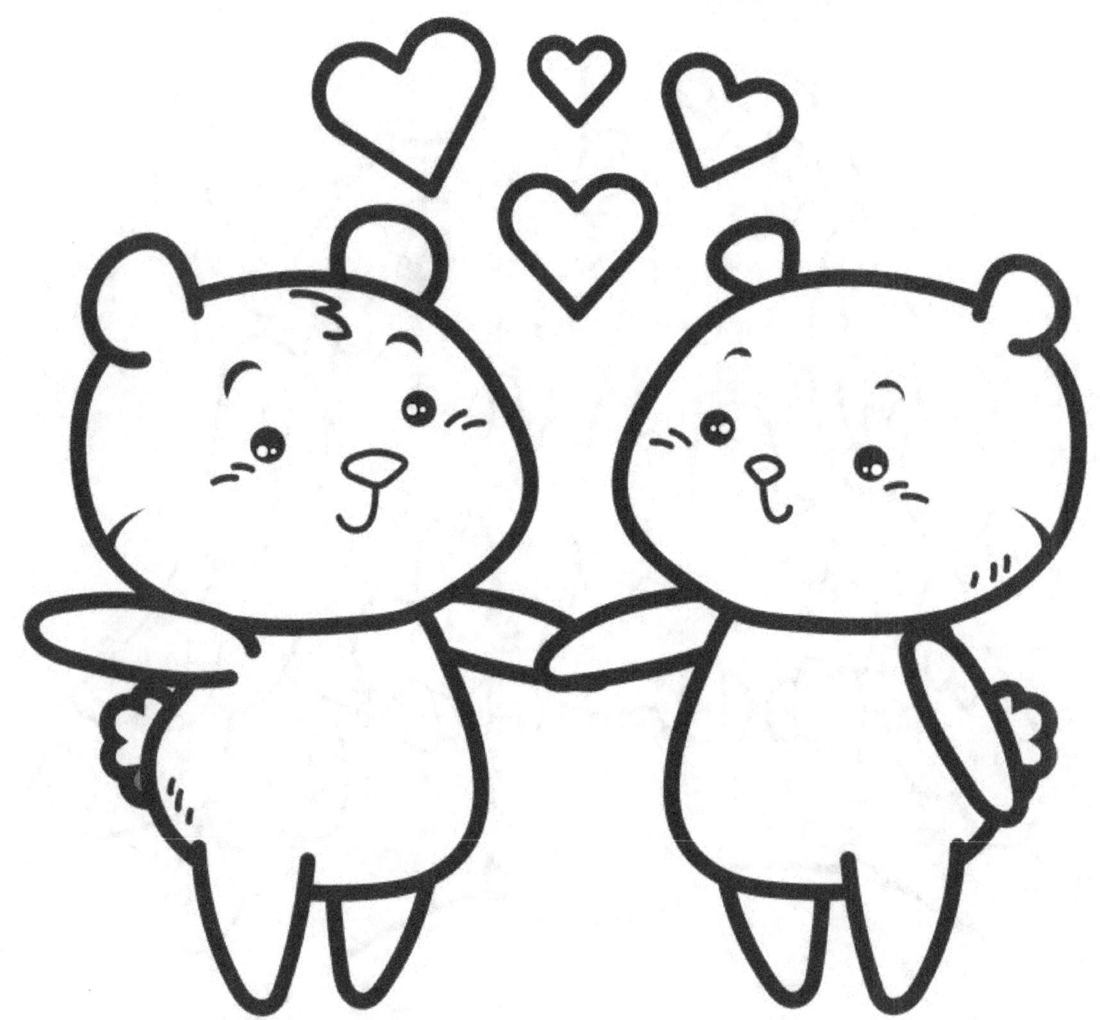

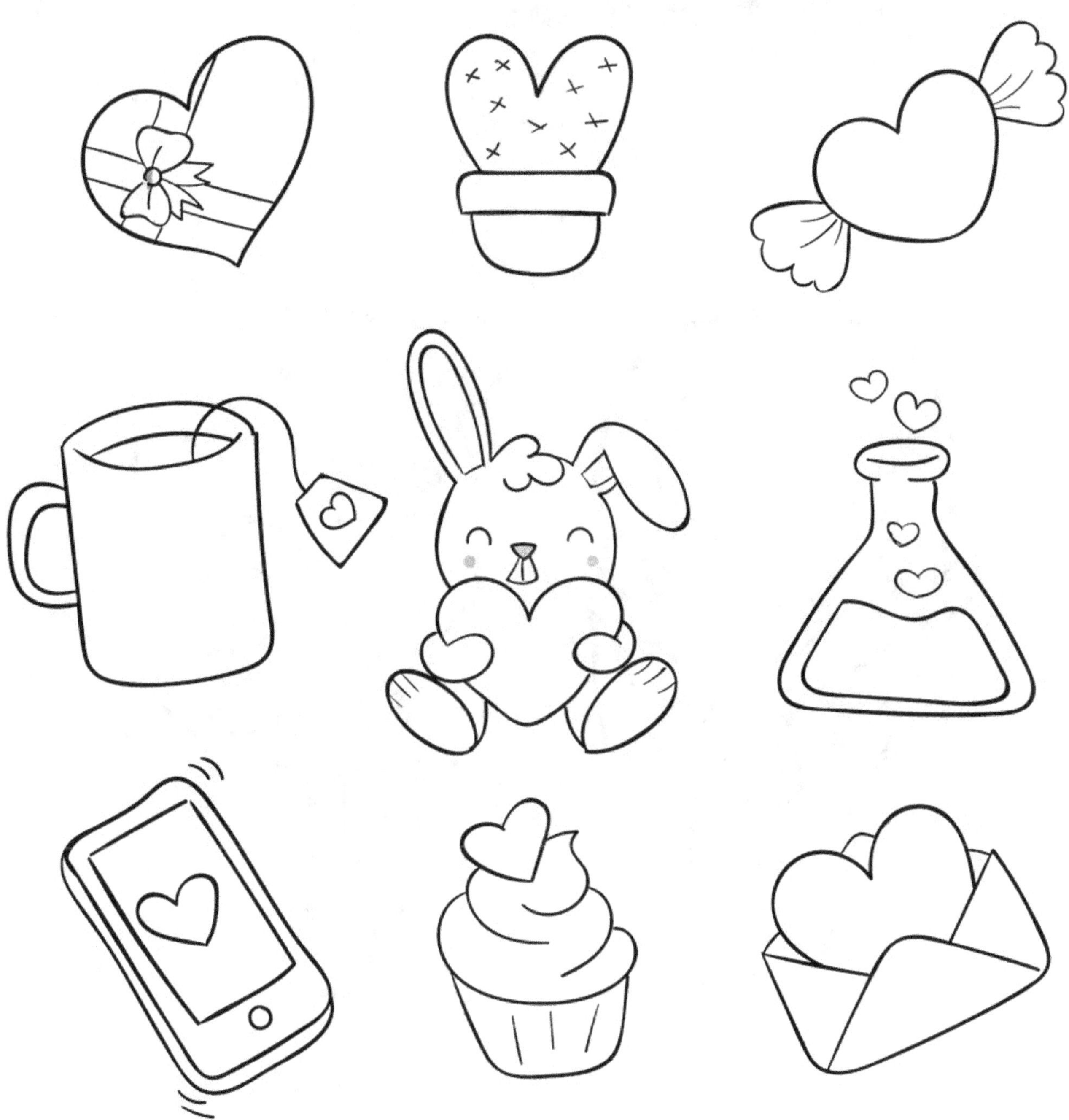

i LOVE

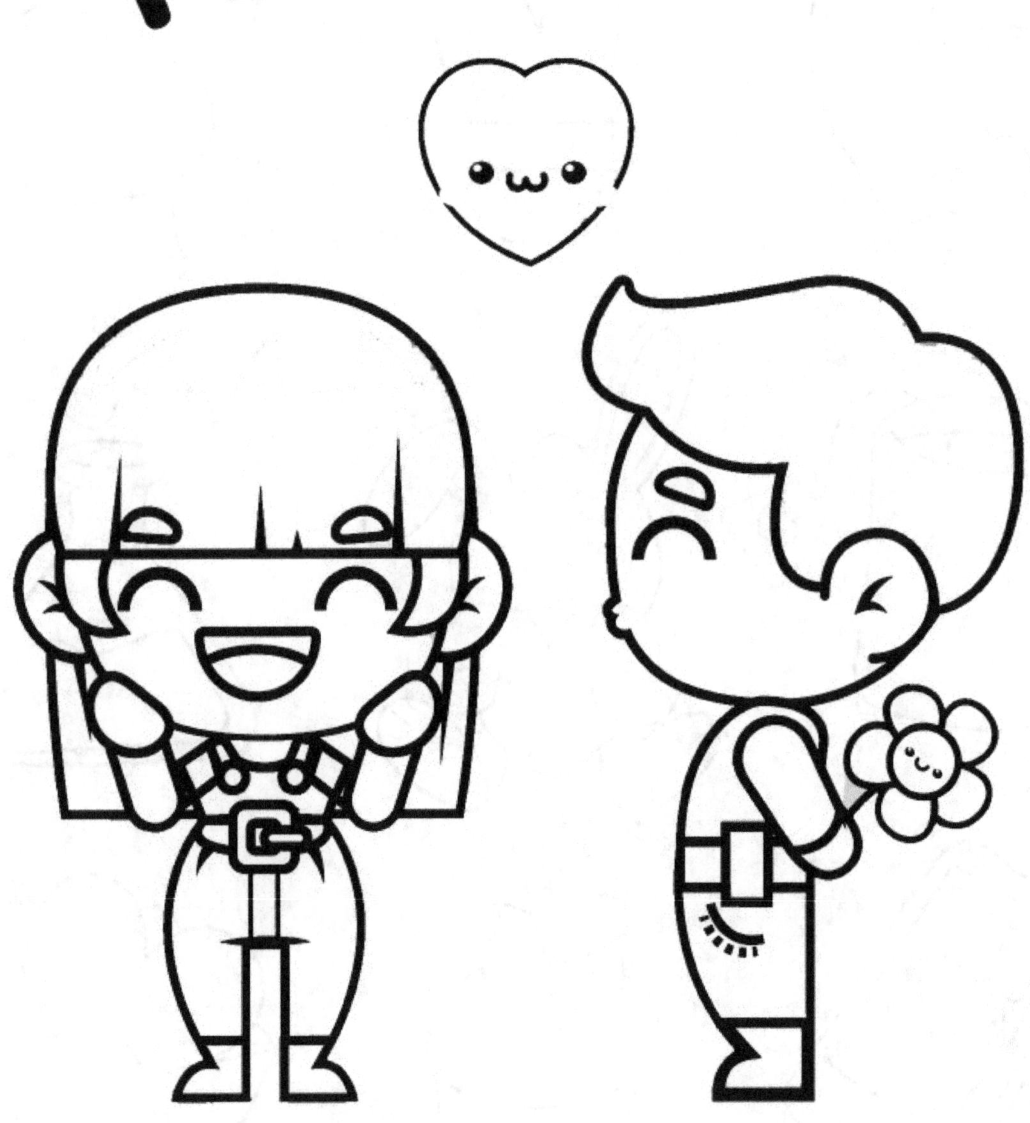

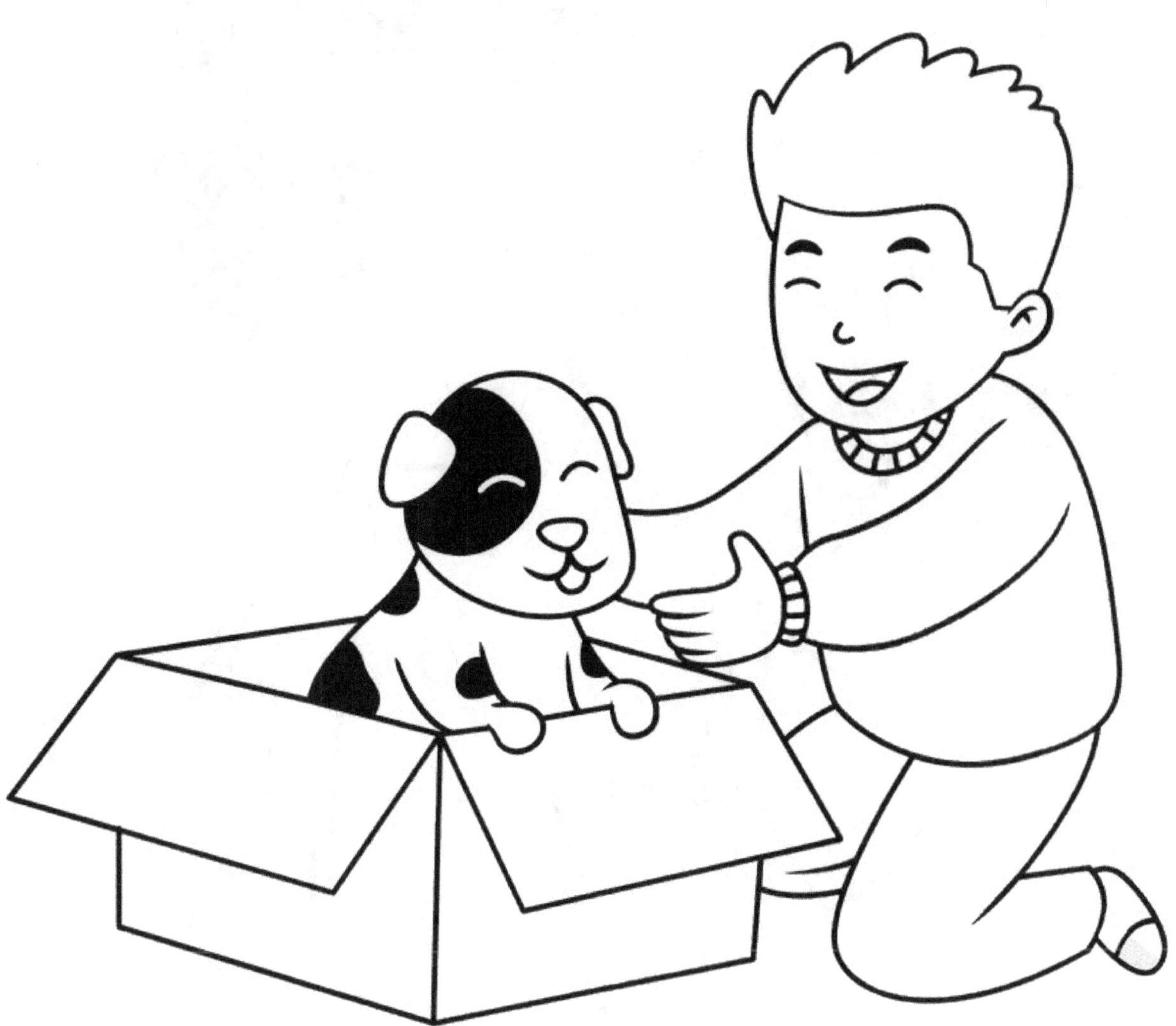

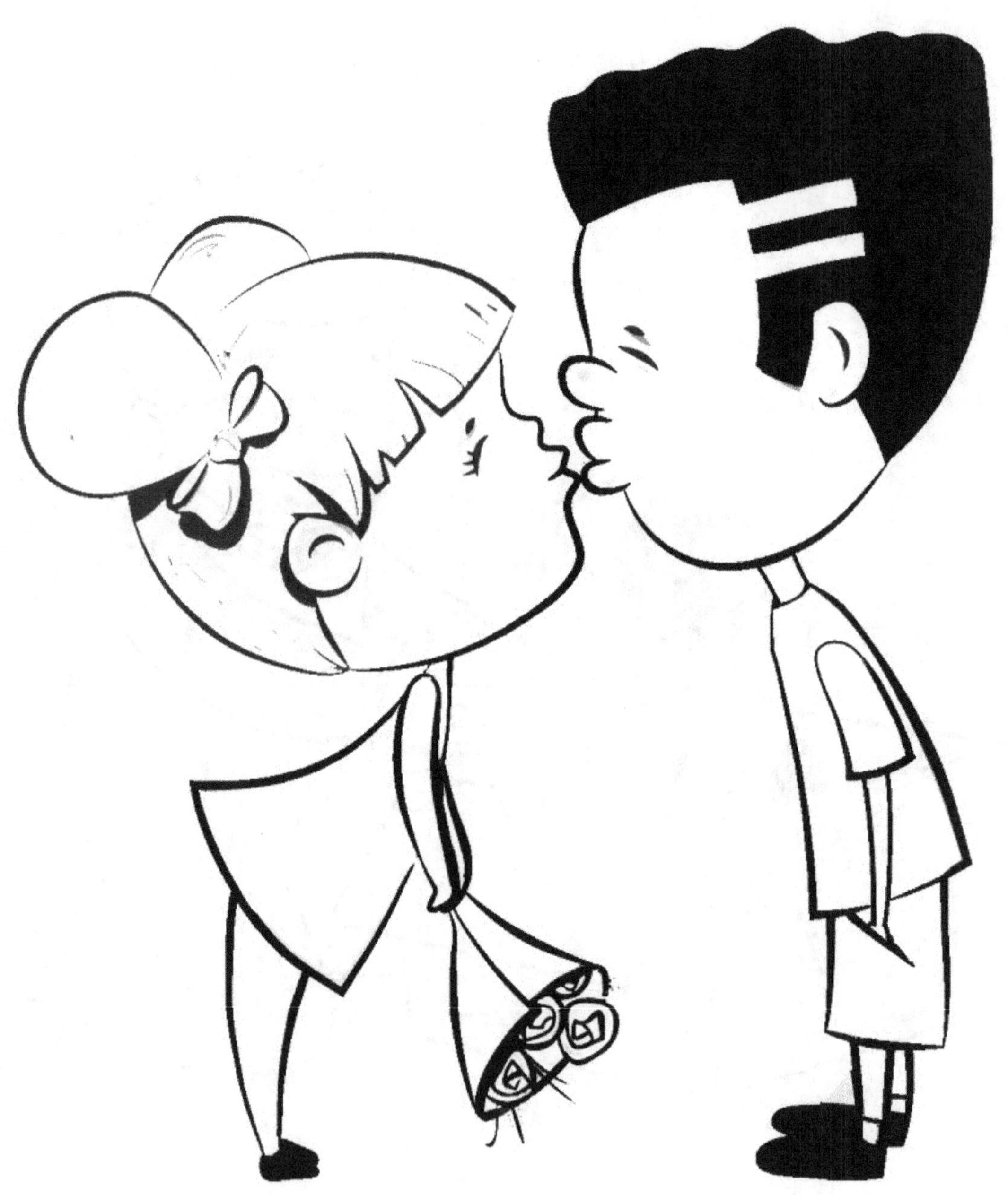

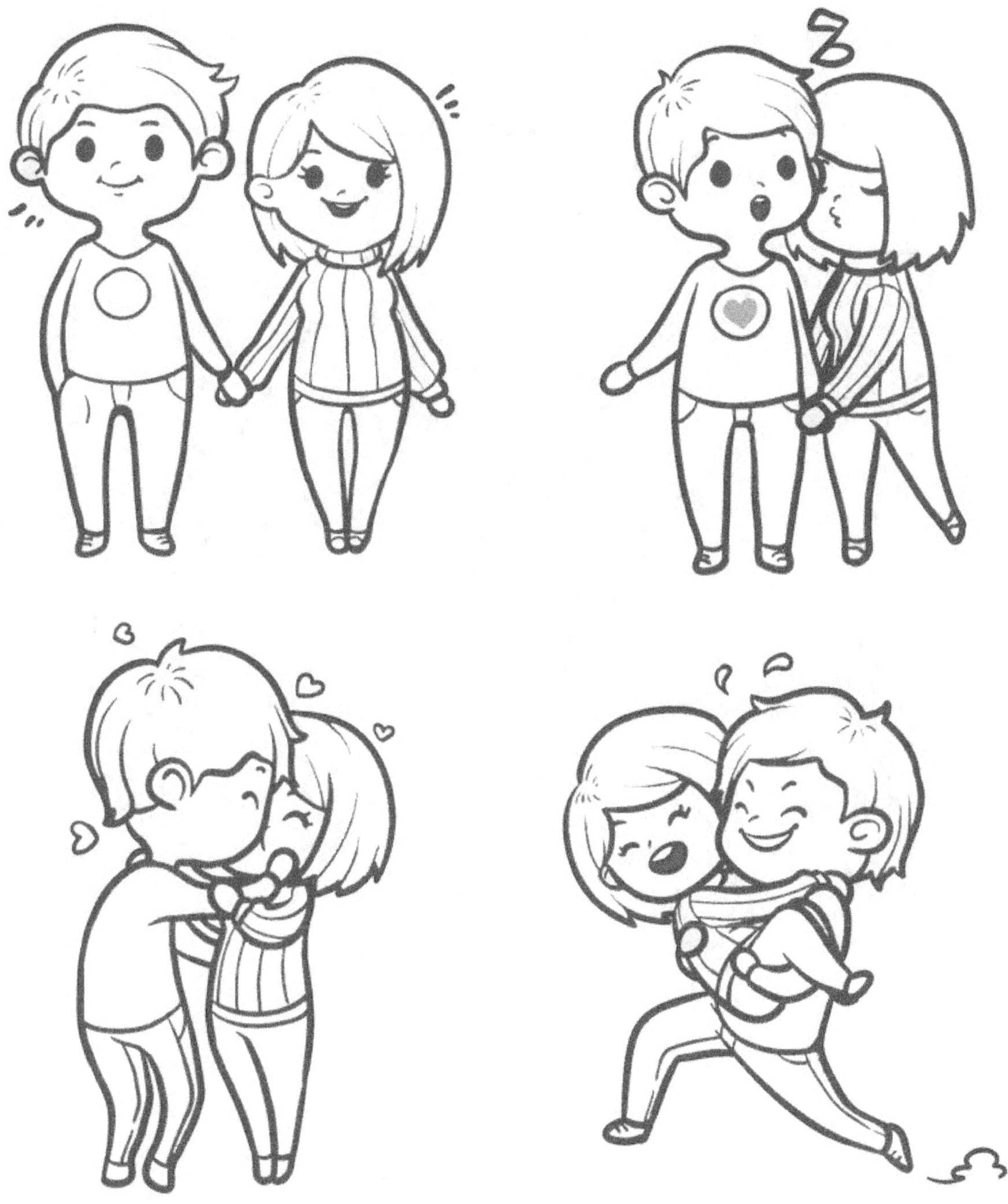

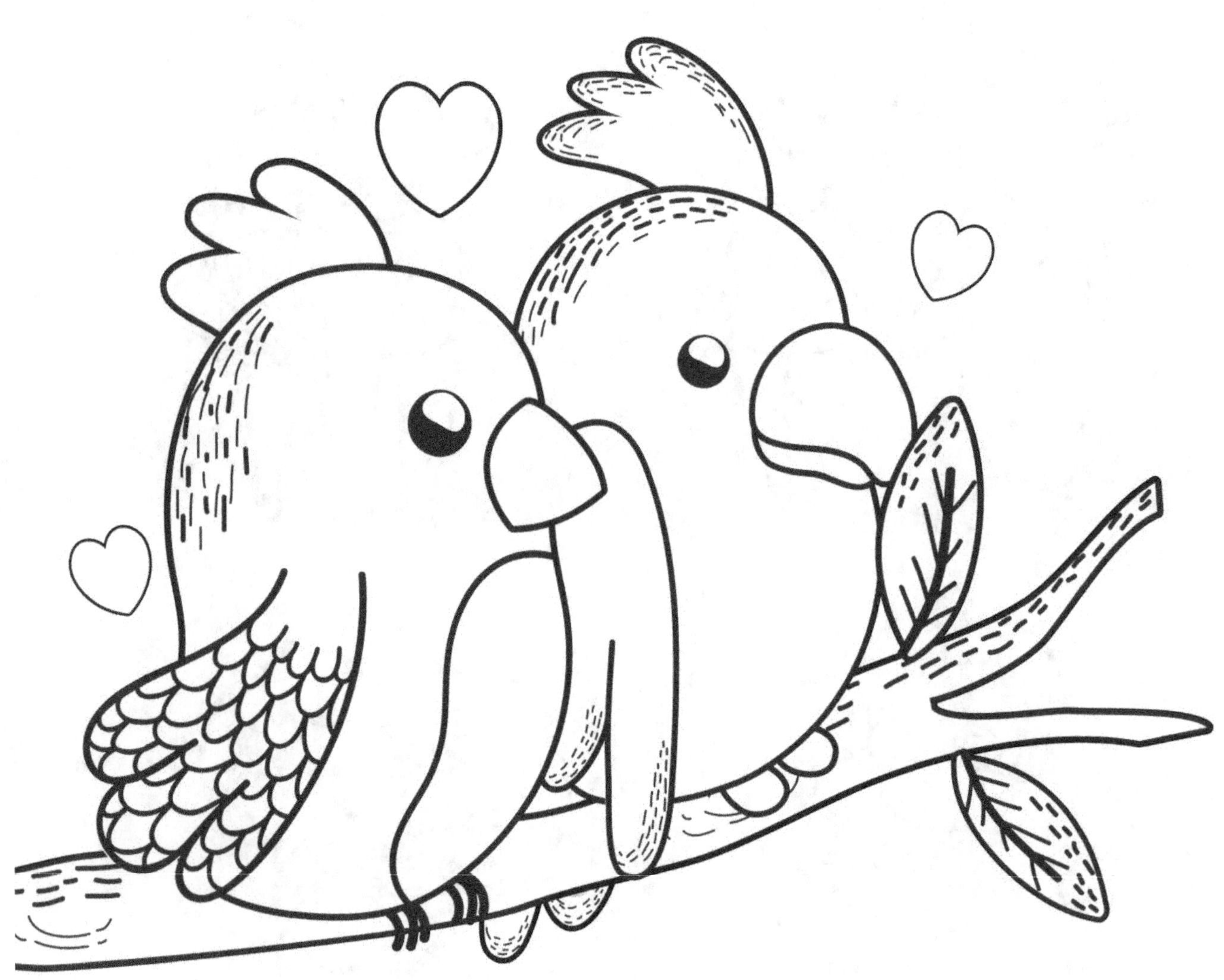

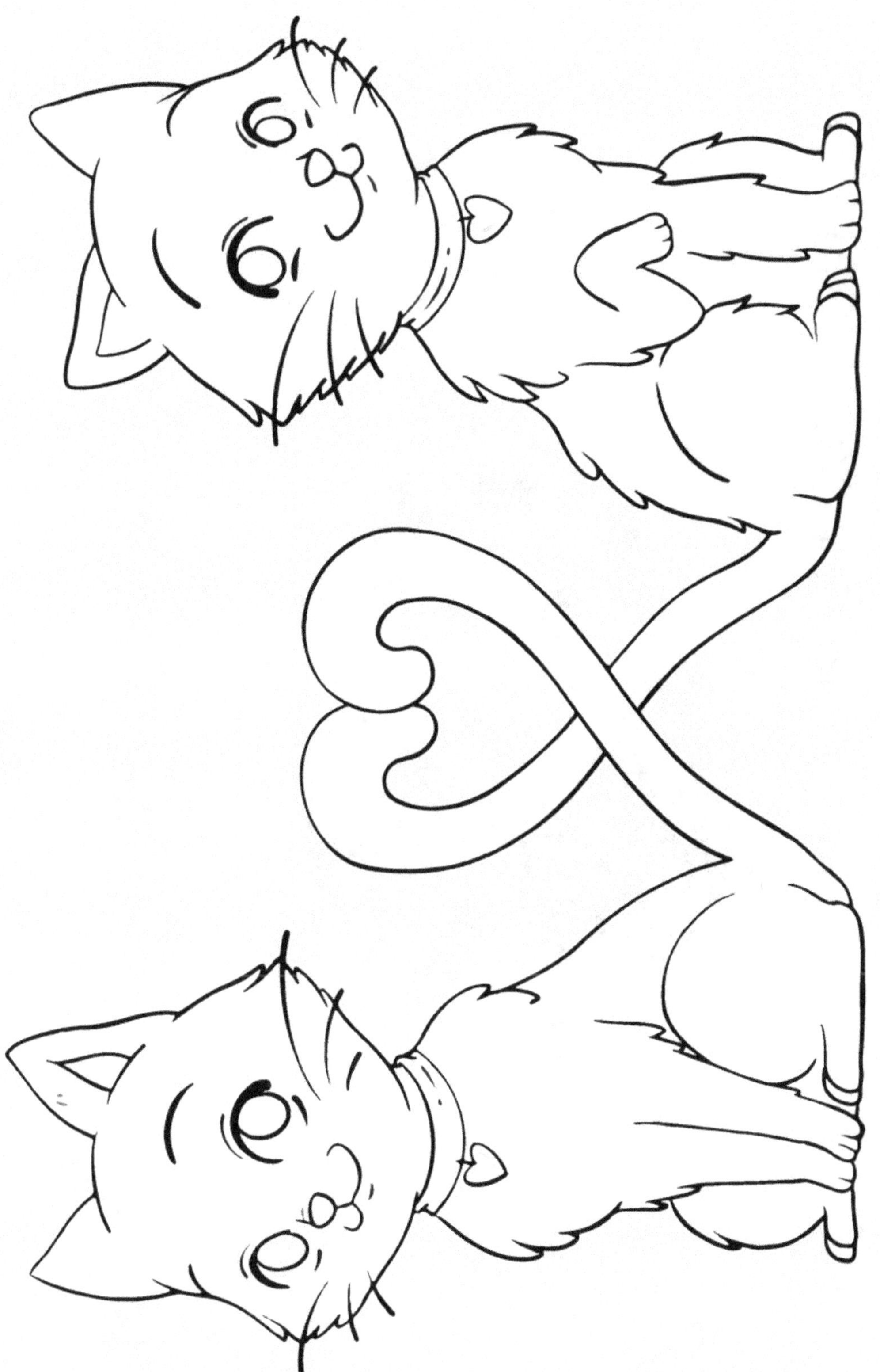

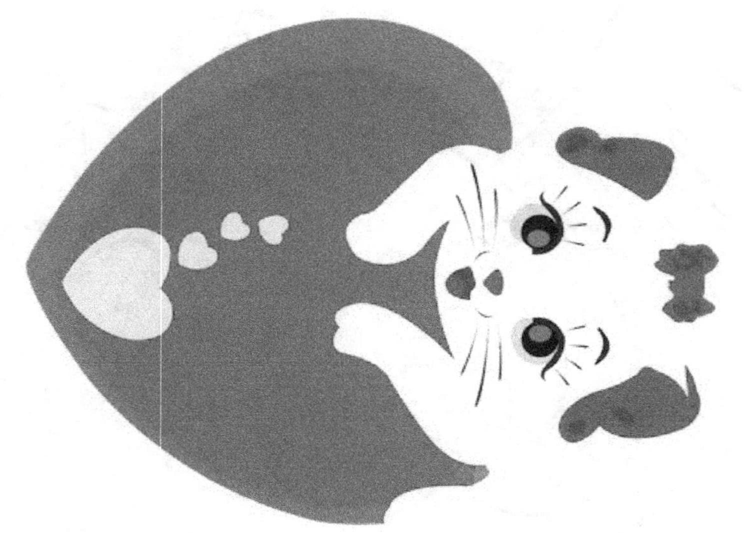

FINISH THE
KITTY YOURSELF

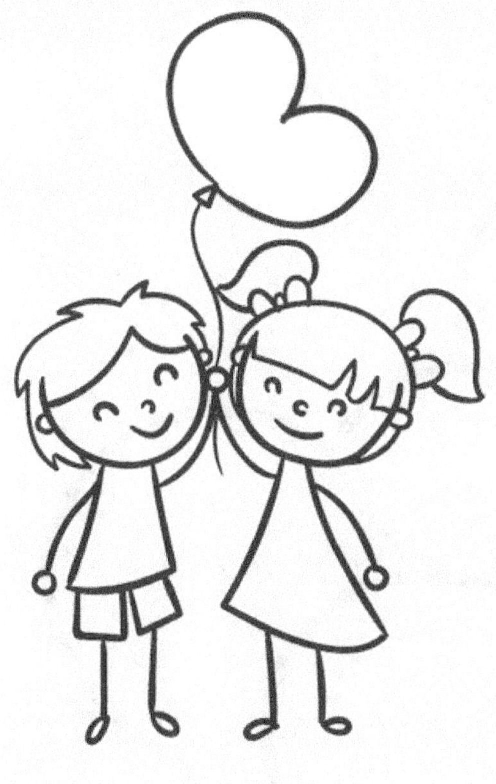

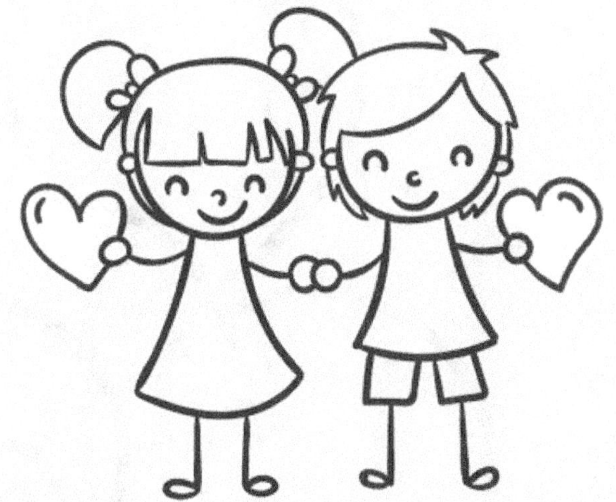

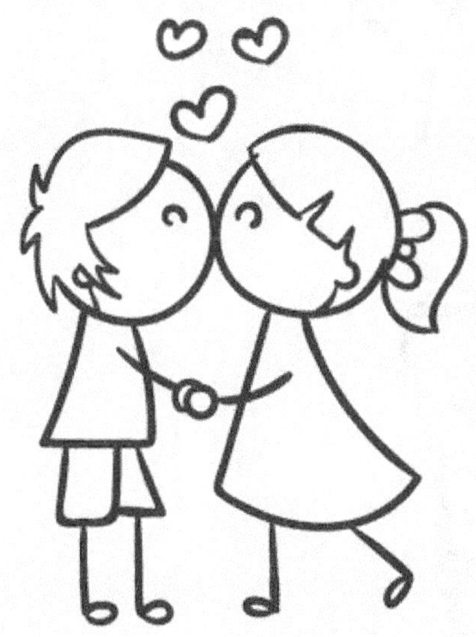

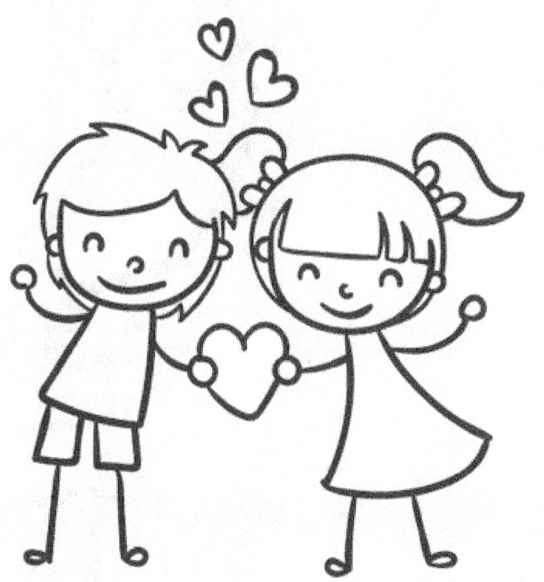

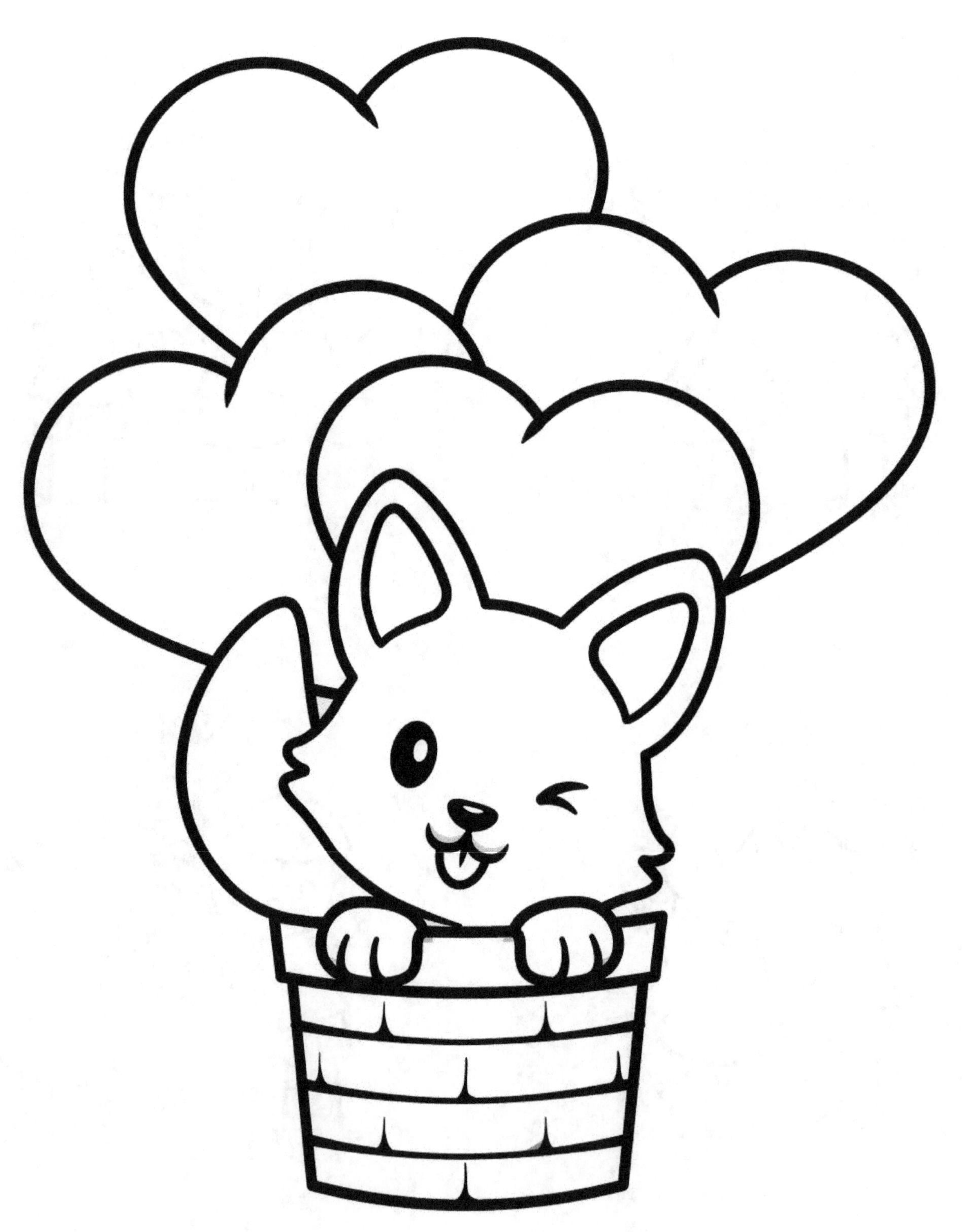

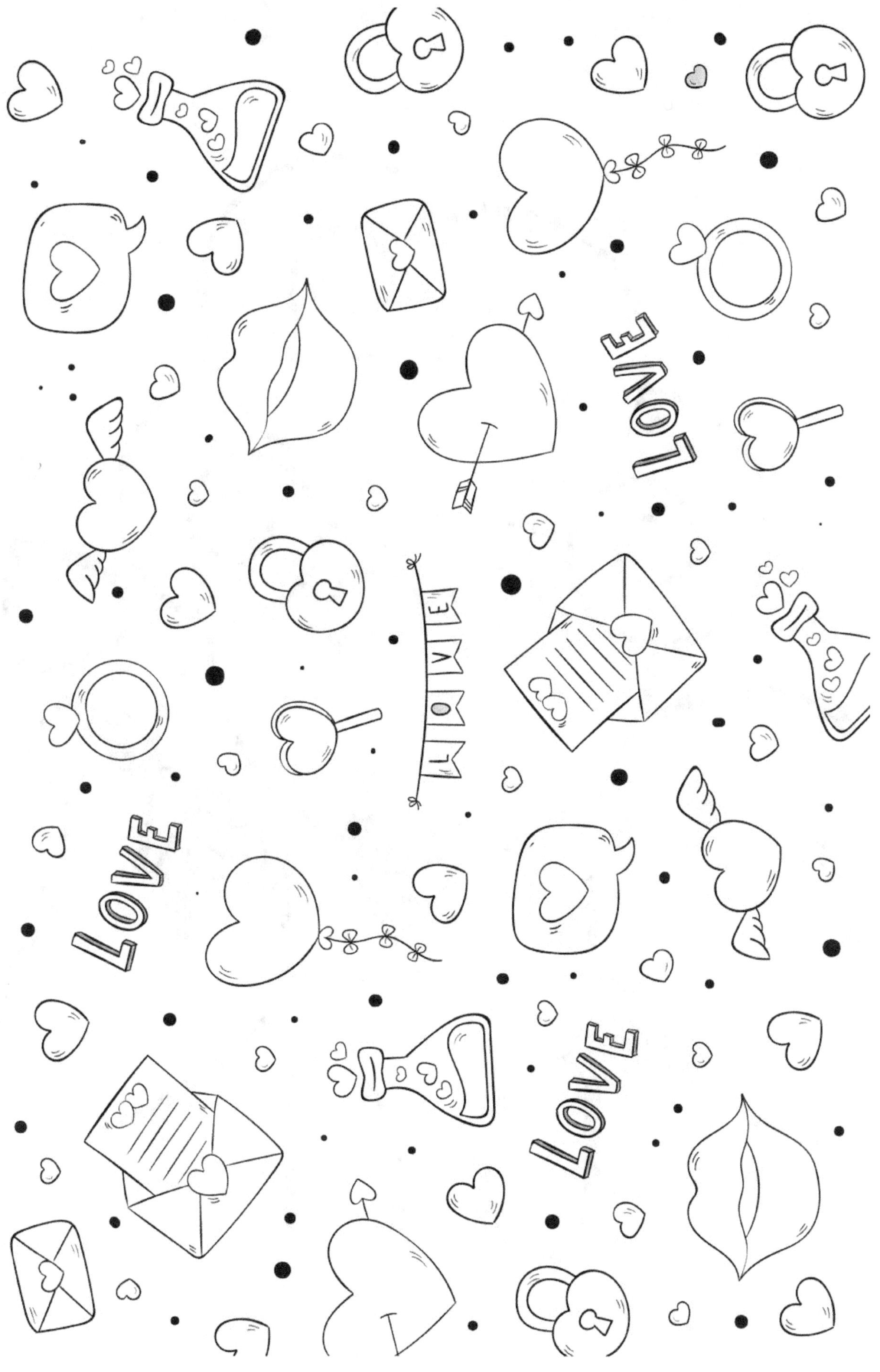

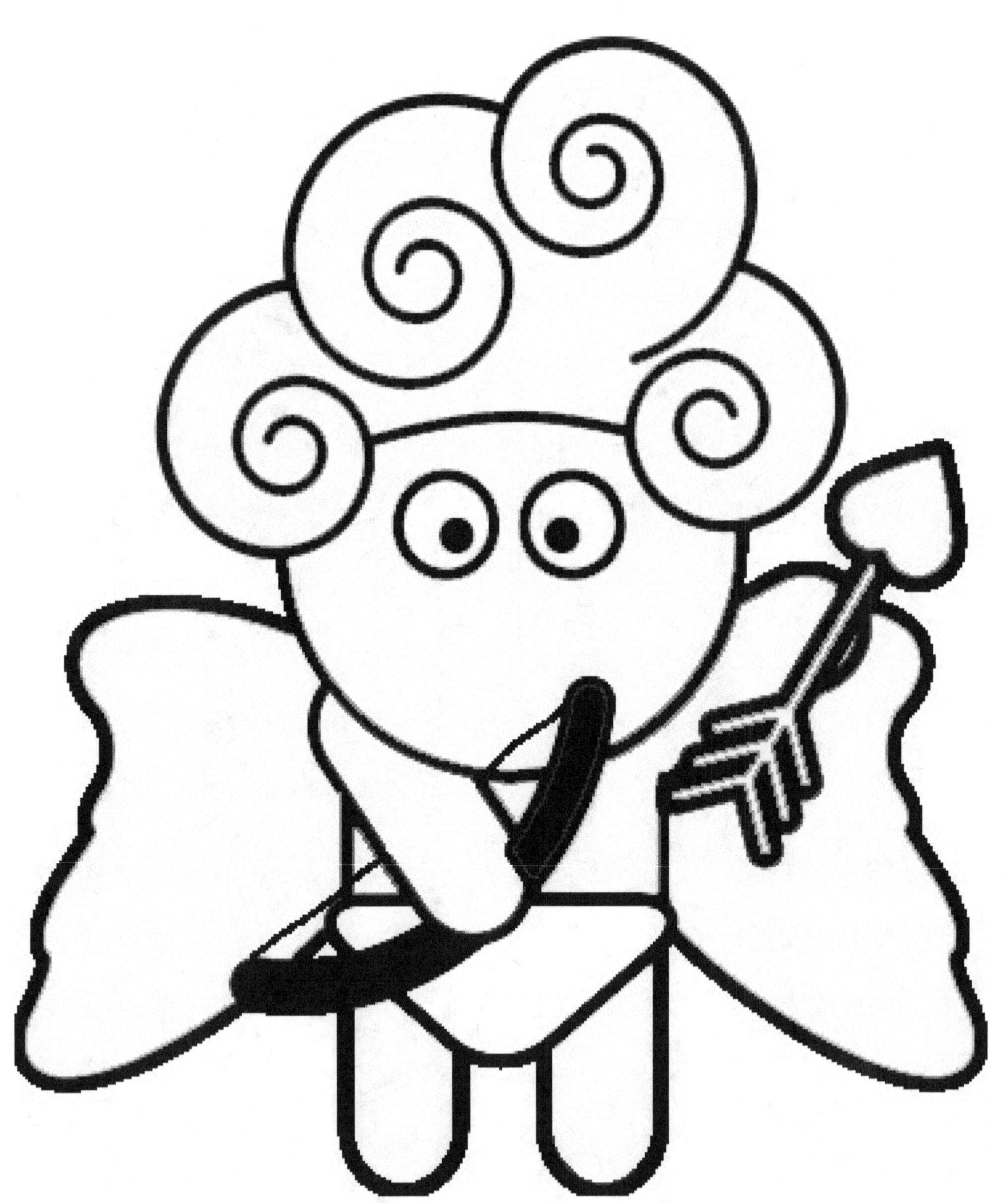

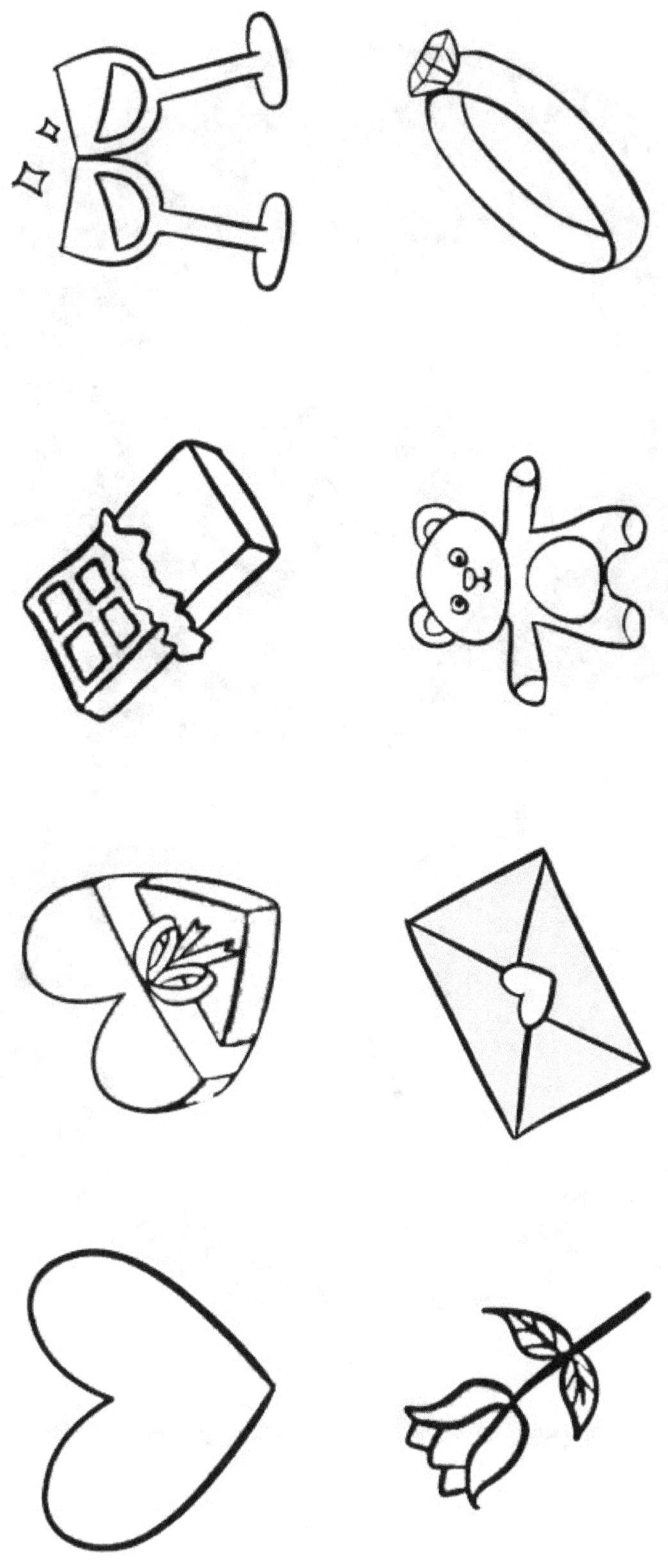

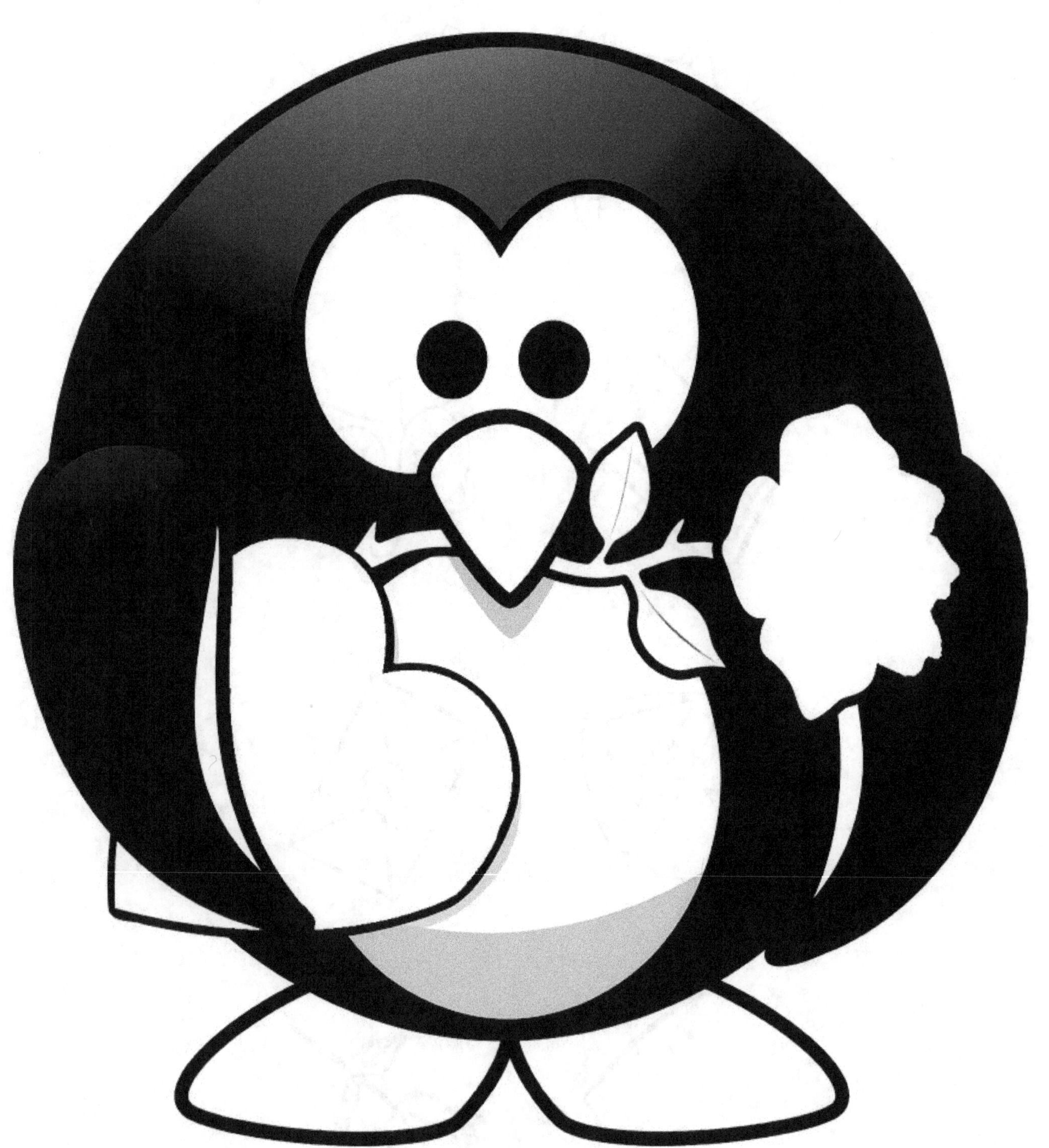

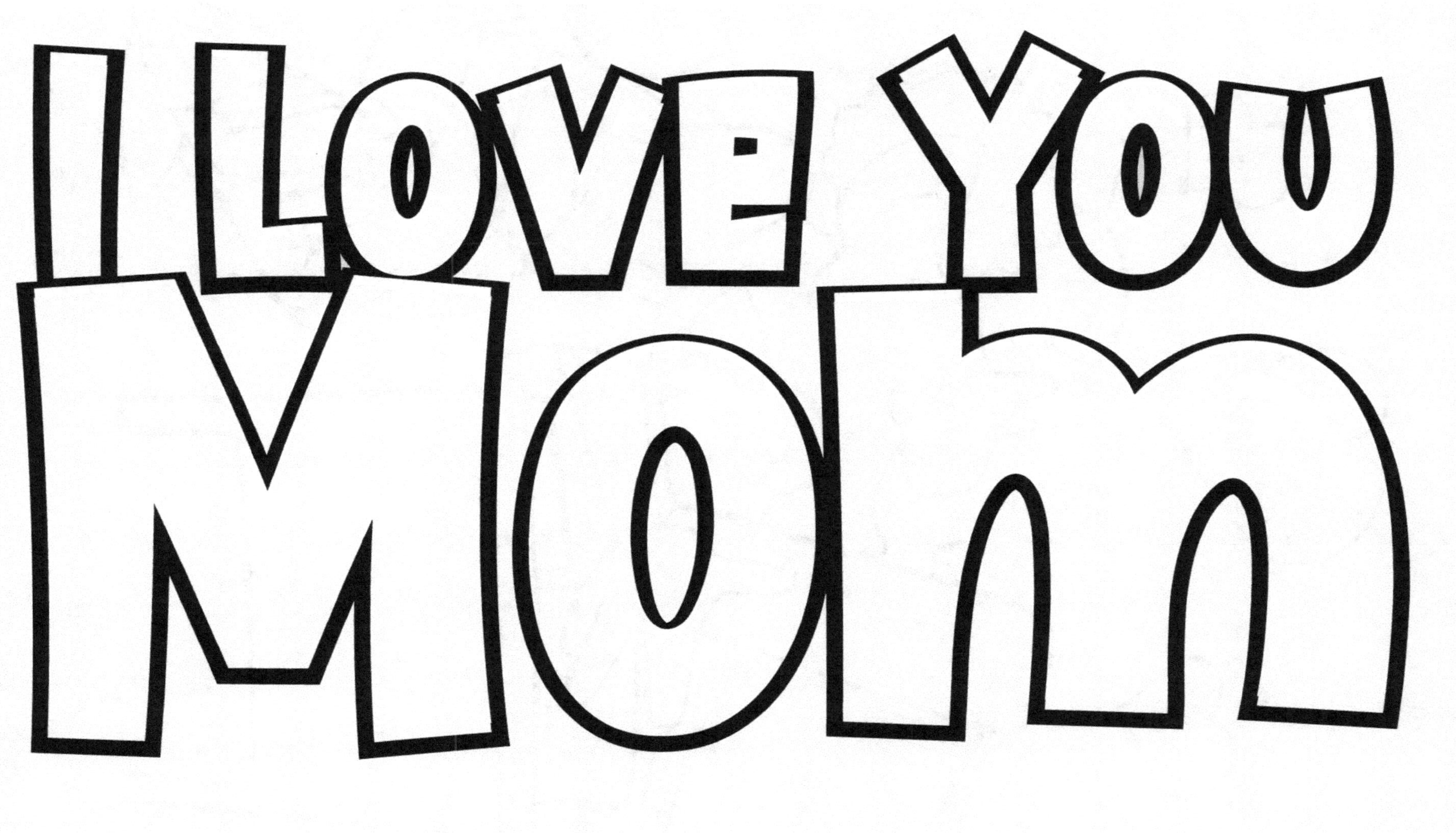
I LOVE YOU Mom

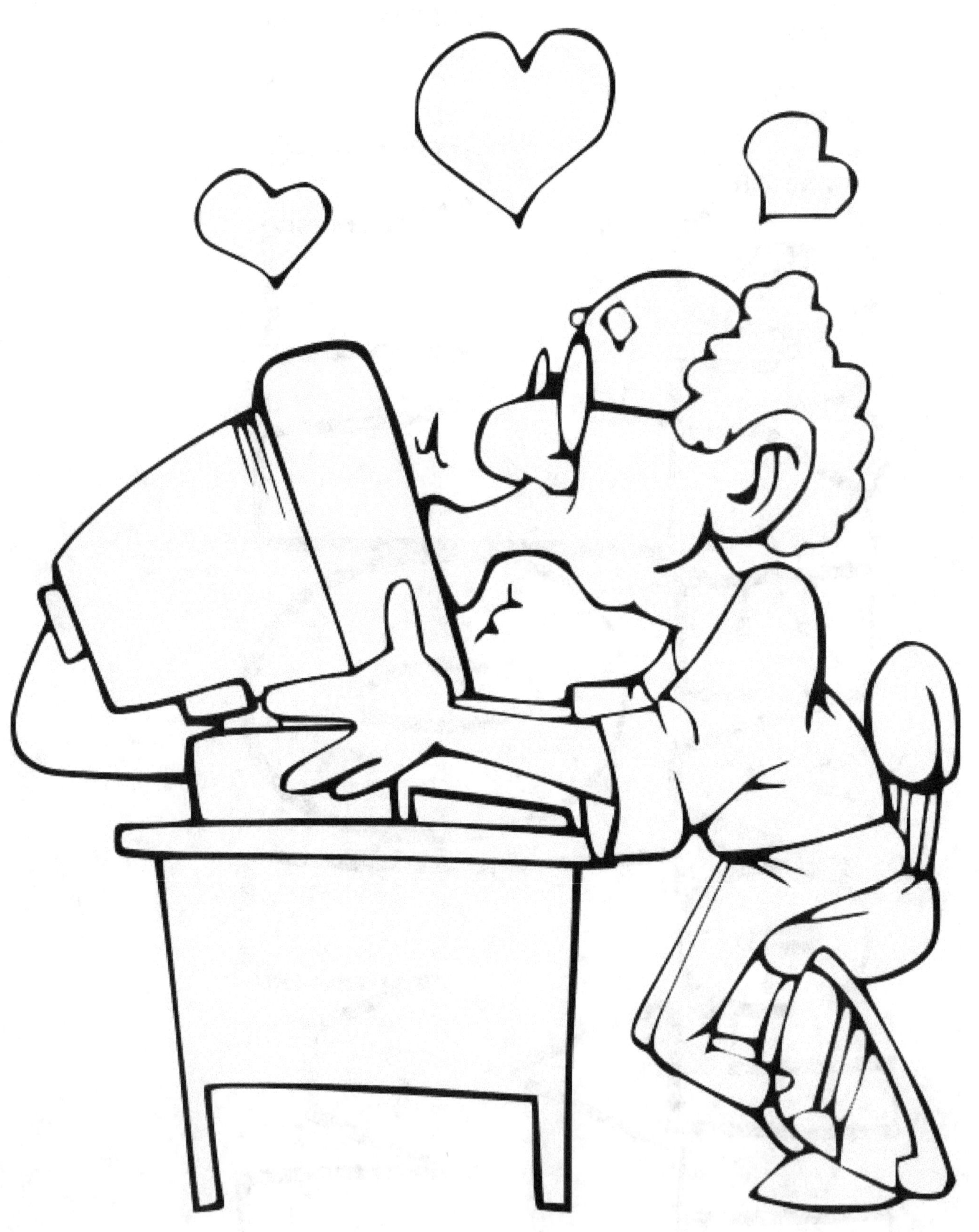

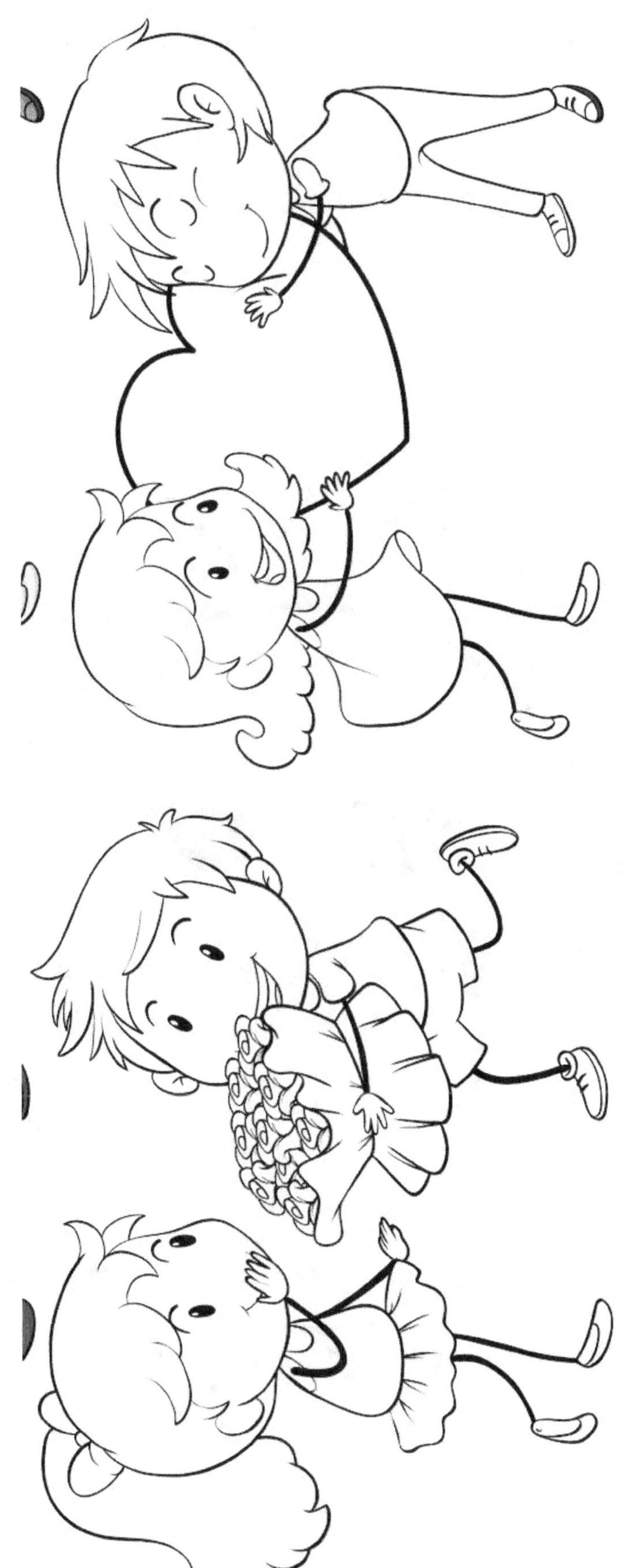

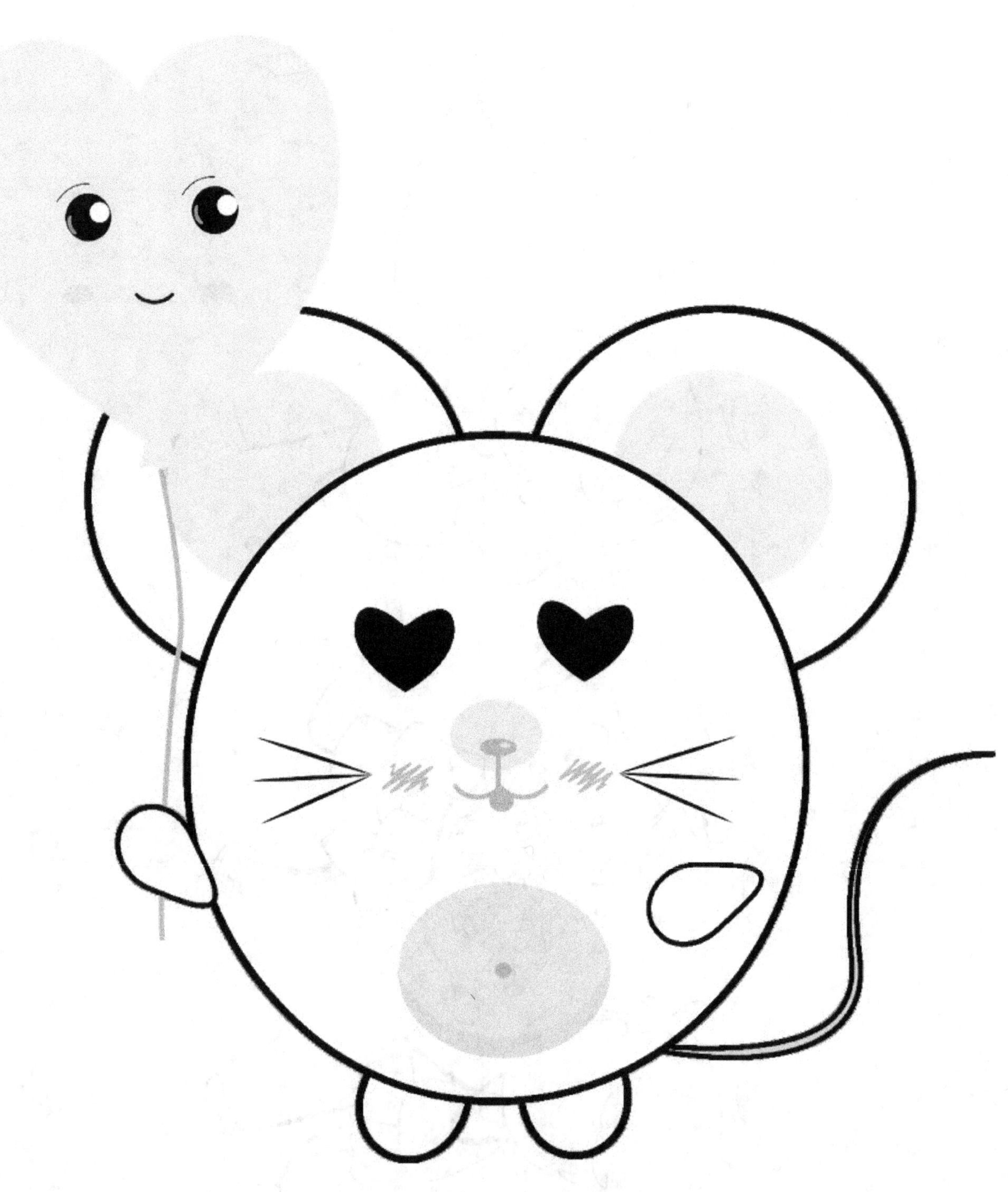

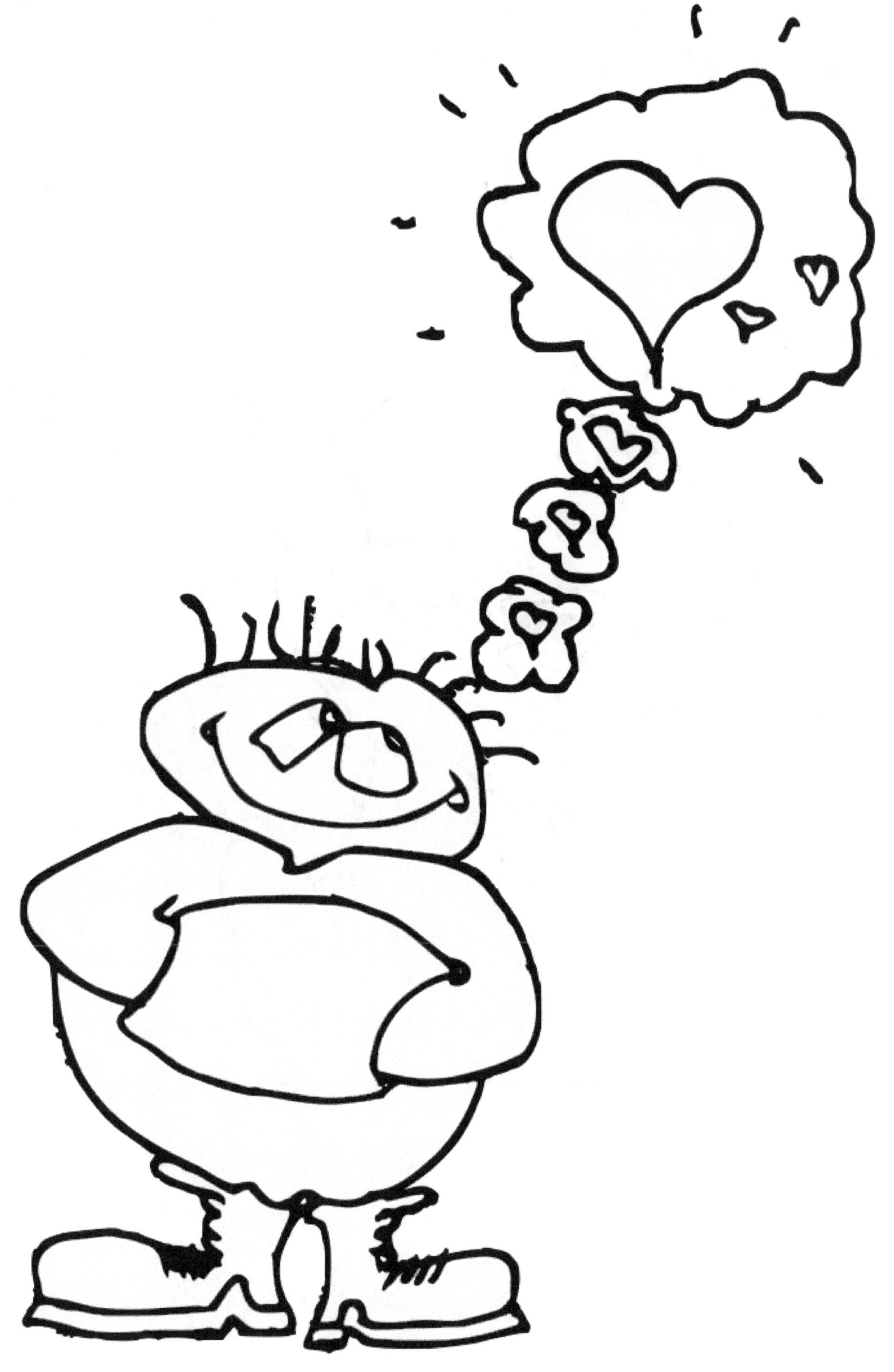

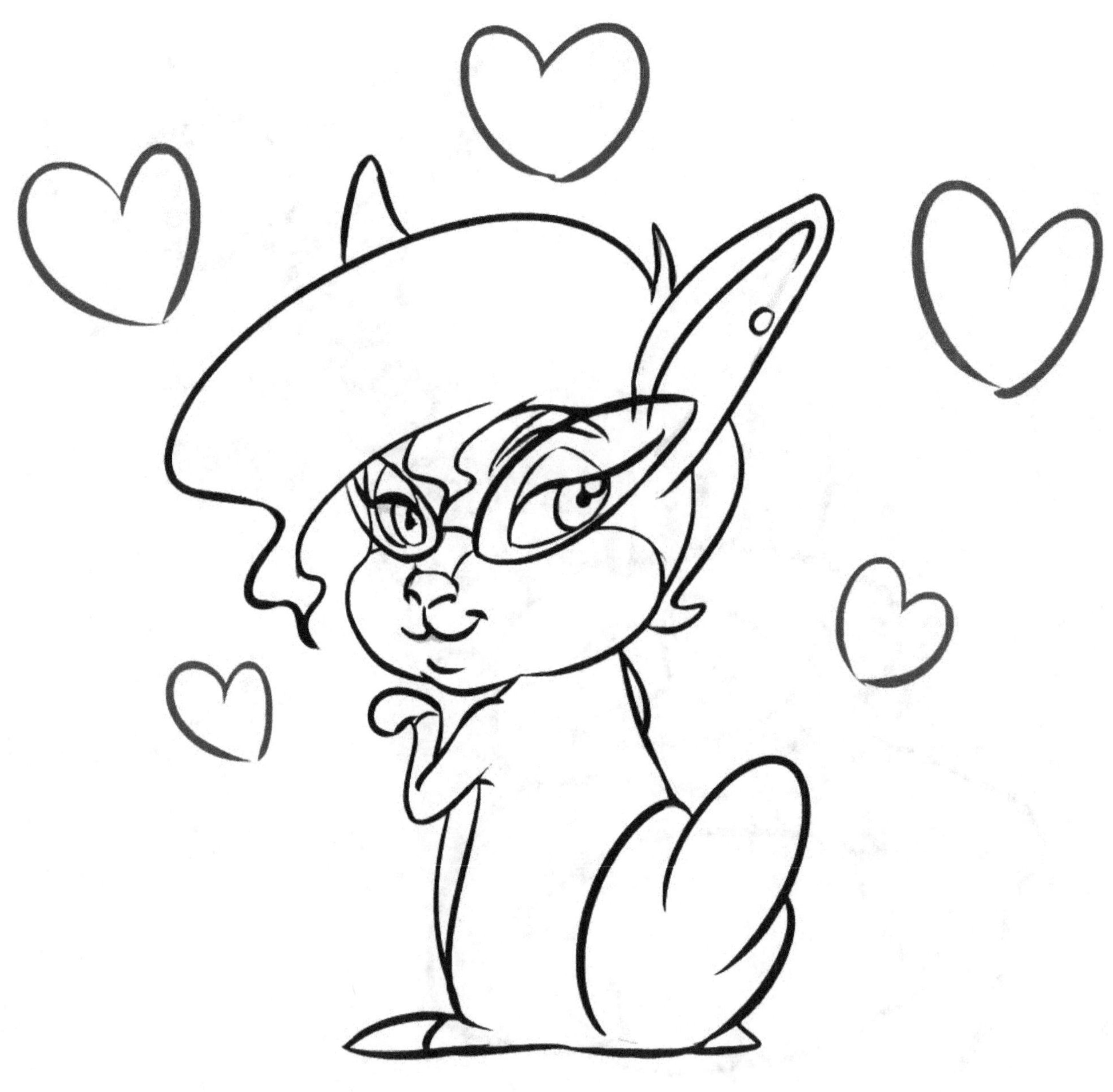

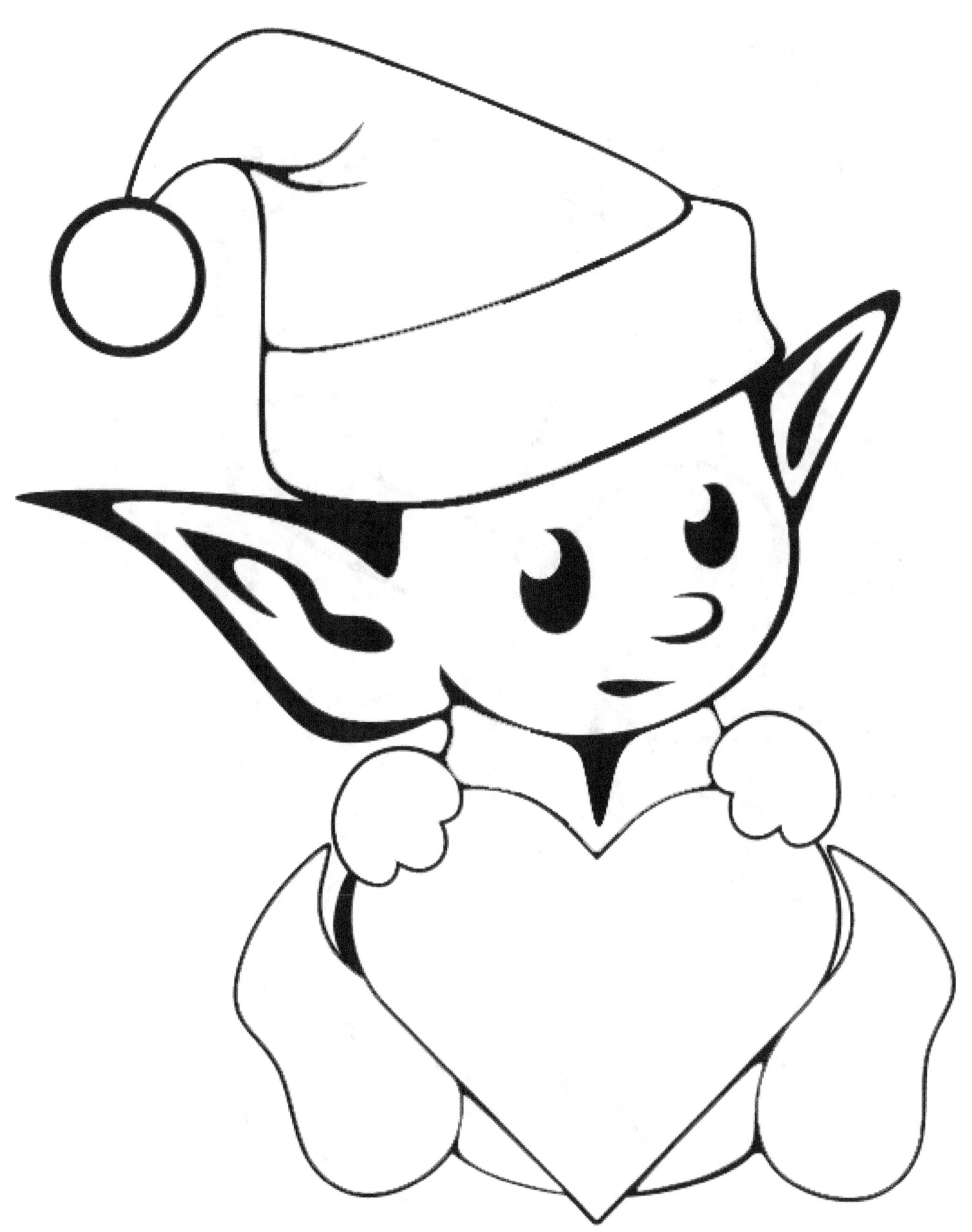

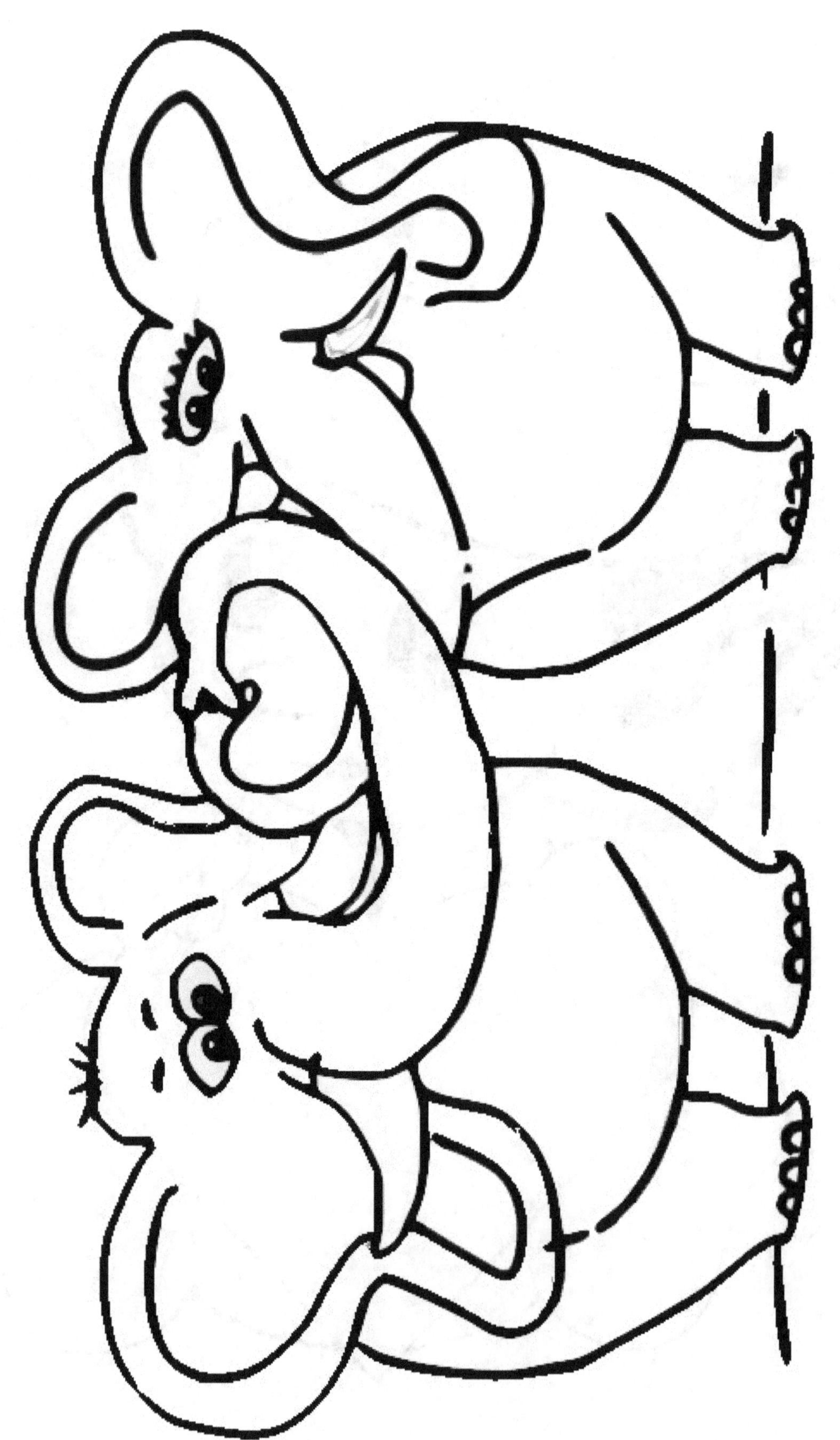

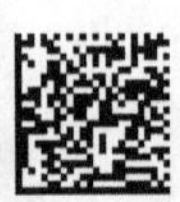

www.ingramcontent.com/pod-product-compliance
Lightning Source LLC
Chambersburg PA
CBHW081324250726
48662CB00008B/2735